Weber

The Illustrated Lives of the Great Composers.

Weber

Anthony Friese-Greene

OMNIBUS PRESS

LONDON · NEW YORK · SYDNEY

Cover design and art direction by Pearce Marchbank Studio
Cover photography by Julian Hawkins

Design and Production in association with
Book Production Consultants,
47 Norfolk Street, Cambridge CB1 2LE

Typeset by Anglia Photoset Ltd, Colchester, Essex
Printed and bound in Singapore by Kyodo Printing Co (S'pore) Pte Ltd.

© Anthony Friese-Greene 1991
This edition published in 1991 by Omnibus Press, a division of Book Sales Ltd.

All pictures from Bildarchiv Preussischer Kulturbesitz except:

National Portrait Gallery, London, 140.
Pictorial Press, 139.
Royal College of Music, 114.
Sachsische Landesbibliothek, 9, 82.
Staatsbibliothek Berlin, 75, 101.

Hardback
Order No. OP44932
ISBN 0.7119.1628.4

Softback
Order No. OP45665
ISBN 0.7119.2081.8

Exclusive Distributors:
Book Sales Limited,
8/9 Frith Street,
London W1V 5TZ

Music Sales Corporation
225 Park Avenue South
New York, NY10003, USA

Music Sales Pty Ltd.,
120 Rothschild Avenue,
Rosebery, NSW 2018, Australia

To the Music Trade only:
Music Sales Limited,
8/9 Frith Street,
London W1V 5TZ

Contents

Chapter 1

Background

When Carl Maria von Weber was born in 1786, Europe was in tumult. Although the French Revolution was still three years off, the gathering storm was already beginning to be felt far beyond the French borders. In Germany, Frederick the Great had died in his armchair at Sanssouci, leaving Prussia in somewhat loose control over 300 independent sovereignties, church states and free cities – politically the country was at a low ebb. Another 85 years were to elapse before the emergence of a fully integrated Germany.

The intellectual life, however, in both France and Germany was at fever pitch. Such had been the far-reaching effect of *Discourses*, the work of French writer and philosopher Jean-Jacques Rousseau, with its new questioning spirit and championing of the importance of the individual, that in Germany he was looked upon almost as a god. In Germany itself, such literary giants as Goethe, Schiller and Lessing were focusing attention on the changing climate of opinion as reflected by the writers of the day. Goethe himself remarked in 1790: 'Knights, robbers, an honest tiers état and an infamous nobility – such are the ingredients of our novels and plays during the last ten years.'

In music, the Classical period was scaling new heights. The last outpouring of celebrated symphonies by Haydn, commencing with the 'Paris' set was under way, whilst Mozart, with the May 1786 production of *The Marriage of Figaro*, was entering the final period of his short life, a period which was to see the composition of his other operatic masterpieces *Don Giovanni*, *Così fan Tutte* and *The Magic Flute*. Beethoven, however, was only a star on the horizon – barely 16 years old when Weber was born.

The birth of Carl Maria Friedrich Ernst von Weber in Eutin, Germany, was originally thought to have taken place on 18 December 1786 at 10.30pm, with the baptism on the 20th, according to a note in the handwriting of his father, Franz Anton. However, it is quite clear from the register in the *Kirchenbüro* in

Jean-Jacques Rousseau
(c. 1740)

The house in Eutin where Weber was born in 1786.

Eutin that the baptismal date is 20 November, indicating that the birth was on 18 November – a month earlier than Franz Anton had recorded. Although the composer's son and biographer, Max Maria, took the view that Franz Anton's entry was the correct one, it is now accepted that the birth took place in November. Uncertainty remains as to whether it was the 18th or 19th.

Eutin lies some six miles inland from the Baltic Sea, more or less equidistant between Kiel and Lübeck. It is an attractive little town boasting more than Weber for its claim to fame; it is also the gateway to the lake district known as 'Holstein Switzerland'. Nowadays you can take a popular Five Lakes Tour from the town, though as the modern travel guide reminds us, you won't see anything remotely resembling an Alp. Eutin has also long been famous for its rose cultivation.

When Weber's father, Franz Anton, came to settle in Eutin in 1779 he was already 45 years old. Having been the Musical Director of the Lübeck Theatre he now took up the post of *Kapellmeister* to the Prince Bishop of Lübeck, whose palace still borders the lake close to the centre of Eutin.

Franz Anton, born in 1734, was one of three sons born to Fridolin and Maria Weber. Their eldest son, Fridolin II, became the father of Constanze Weber, who later became the wife of Wolfgang Amadeus Mozart. Both Franz Anton and his brother Fridolin were 'inspired by the spirit of music, or rather possessed by it, as if by a mocking demon' writes Max Maria 'which, by its fascination, was ever leading them astray upon their troubled path of life.' This was certainly true for Franz Anton, who

Franz Anton von Weber.

Karl Theodor, Elector of the Palatinate.

was strikingly handsome, reckless in spirit, and jovial in manner.

From an early age the two brothers showed unusual musical talent. Franz Anton played the violin and both brothers sang. It is said that their musical prowess came to the ears of Karl Theodor, the Elector of the Palatinate, who invited them to Mannheim, where he had established an opera troupe and orchestra renowned for their excellence. In the case of Fridolin II, this artistic milieu seems to have been congenial for only a short period. With Franz Anton it was to be different – the stage, or the travelling theatre, was to present a recurring lure for him throughout his chequered life. But Franz Anton was also eager at this time to pursue a military career, and a commission was given to him as ensign in the Elector's guard, provided that he did not withdraw his services from the operatic stage of Mannheim. However, this did not suit the restless Franz Anton, and, having risen in favour with General

9

Baron von Weichs, the Commander of the forces of the Electorate, Max Maria tells us 'he flung aside opera scores and instrument, and followed his new protector into the imperial army.' In an ensuing campaign, his foolhardiness won him the admiration of his fellow soldiers. However, at the battle of Rossbach he is said to have been wounded. This was probably the signal for another change of direction and he left military service. Through the recommendation of Baron von Weichs, who appears to have had a fatherly affection for him, he entered the civil service of Clemens August, Elector of Cologne and Bishop of Hildesheim.

The change was destined to affect his personal life, for Franz Anton's new job required him to come into contact with a certain financial Court Councillor called Fumetti, who held the steward-ship of Steuerwald. He had a daughter, Maria Anna, whose beauty was not lost on Franz Anton, and his affection for her was soon returned. He married her in 1758. Divine providence smiled on Franz Anton at this point in his life, for not only did Maria Anna's father die, leaving a considerable fortune to the young couple, but his death meant that the way was clear for Franz Anton to assume Fumetti's lucrative appointment! Apparently, a decree existed that carried with it the understanding that Maria Anna should marry a man of good report, so that her husband might be appointed steward on her father's death. Although little was known about Franz Anton by the good burghers of Hildesheim (and strong objections were lodged), the Elector insisted that the appointment was confirmed. Extraordinary as it may seem, given his somewhat wayward character, Franz Anton held this position for ten years. His dismissal in 1768 was not the doing of the Elector Clemens August, but of his successor, Bishop Friedrich Wilhelm, who was much less inclined to overlook the eccentric and erratic behaviour of the young civil servant. As Max Maria records, Franz Anton 'had indulged his passion for music to such a pitch of fanaticism that he was always to be seen playing his violin in public, sometimes marching at the head of his numerous progeny, sometimes wielding his bow in the fields; while the office papers lay around in dusty confusion.'

At about this time, Franz Anton began to call himself 'von Weber', even though the Elector's decrees only referred to him as plain 'Weber'. In his biography of the composer, John Warrack convincingly counters any claims the Weber family had to a title of nobility, and at the same time argues that Franz Anton was responsible for the 'von' being interpolated. 'Clearly he encour-aged everyone', writes Warrack, 'even within his family circle to regard him as noble: Carl Maria inherited the belief in perfectly good faith, and his aunt Adelheid, Franz Anton's sister, styled herself Baroness. It is thus through usage, not inheritance, that the composer retains his "von".'

Maria Anna bore Franz Anton eight children and, following a long period of suffering, died in 1783, four years after Franz Anton was appointed *Kapellmeister* at Eutin. Her life had not been an easy one, and the fortune she brought him on her marriage had been mostly squandered. Her death seems to have rekindled all Franz Anton's restlessness and in 1784, the following year, we find him in Vienna handing over his sons, Fritz and Franz Edmund, to Haydn as pupils. The astonishing success of Mozart as a young prodigy had excited Franz Anton into thinking that perhaps a similar destiny might be possible for his own sons. But, as is so often the case, destiny chose otherwise, and it was Franz Anton's life which changed most as a result of this action. The home in which his sons were lodged in Vienna belonged to a family called Brenner, and it was here that he met Genovefa, the pretty daughter of the house, who was 21. Franz Anton, now 50, fell violently in love with her and she returned his affection. They were married in 1785. Franz Anton returned to Eutin, not as *Kapellmeister*, as he had been when he was married to his first wife, but in the humble position of town musician. The duties of his office were to conduct the music at court balls and state dinners, and to play at the weddings and serenades of the citizens or farmers. Julius Benedict tells us:

Franz Anton felt the humiliation of his position keenly, but his sufferings were greatly surpassed by the deep melancholy of his pining and home-sick young wife, torn away from gay Vienna and all the friends of her early youth, to vegetate in Eutin, the dullest of provincial towns.

A view of Vienna in the 1750s.

Chapter 2

Early Childhood

Carl Maria von Weber was born in what is now known as Lübecker Strasse, Eutin. He was a sickly child, and was later found to suffer from a disease of the right hip-bone, which caused him to limp throughout his life.

Shortly after his birth we find his father, Franz Anton, bored with the life of town musician and moving to Hamburg: his *Wanderlust* had asserted itself again. What happened now was to have a direct influence on the life and health of young Carl Maria. Franz Anton conceived the idea of going on the road with his family as a group of players called '*von Weberschen Schauspieler-gesellschaft*' (The Weber Theatre Company), consisting of himself, his exhausted and protesting young wife, grown-up daughters from his first marriage, baby Carl Maria, and Franz Anton's sister, Adelheid, who was to prove the one stable and guiding force in the child's early years. At this time, Germany, like other countries, relied for its theatrical entertainment on itinerant groups of actors and musicians. It was, in the main, a hard and unrewarding life, involving long hours of travel and waiting about in the cold – not the ideal environment for a delicate child. Nevertheless, Franz Anton was still intent on 'rearing a second Mozart', as Benedict puts it, 'and not having succeeded with his other sons, he began at once to train the poor boy, who could not walk till he was four years old, though he was taught to put his tiny fingers on the piano and to sing almost before he was able to speak.'

In fact, the child had his first music lesson at the age of three, from his father. Fridolin, his half-brother, apparently tried to teach him some rudiments of violin playing. Weber, in later life, used to relate the story of Fridolin tearing the violin bow from his little trembling hands, striking him with it over the knuckles, and angrily exclaiming 'whatever may be made of you, Carl, it will never be a musician!'

However, for all the disadvantages that the roving life brought for the health of the young boy, and the questionable moral influences to which he was subjected, this period, which lasted some years, acted as a seed-bed for his impressionable mind, 'and gave him', as Max Maria states, 'that dramatic insight and knowledge of theatrical effect, which stood him in such good stead in his operatic compositions.'

The circuit which The Weber Theatre Company took in was in the south of Germany, chiefly round the towns of Erlangen, Nuremberg and Augsburg. As the child of a theatrical manager, Weber's playmates were other actors' children. His woods, meadows and gardens were daubed on canvas: a painted palace was his street. As the composer tells us in a subsequent autobiographical sketch, 'my time was chiefly devoted to painting and music. I was successful in several branches of the former – painting in oils, miniatures and pastel and having some skill in engraving.' (Whilst in Nuremberg Weber had lessons in painting and engraving.) 'But imperceptibly my interest in painting dwindled and was finally ousted by music almost before I was aware of it.'

In 1796 The Weber Theatre Company came to Hildburgs-hausen, about 20 miles from Meiningen. Nine years on the road had taken its toll on Genovefa's health, which had never been good, and Franz Anton was obliged to take a rest from the company for a few weeks, so that his wife might regain her strength. Here, in Hildburgshausen, the young Weber came into contact with 23-year-old composer and musician Johann Peter Heuschkel, of whom he later said, 'To him I owe my firm grounding and my achievement of a powerful, well articulated and characterised piano style, with the equal training of both hands.'

Meanwhile, Franz Anton's company had arrived in Salzburg and, with Genovefa's health showing improvement, the decision was made to rejoin them. Arriving in Salzburg in the autumn of 1797, Franz Anton assumed directorship of his theatrical company and looked forward to a projected tour of Bavaria, Baden and the Palatinate. But the tour was not to be – political storm clouds had been gathering fast. The French Republican armies were sweeping up from the West like a tidal wave. General Moreau already stood before Munich: Napoleon's Italian advance had driven the Austrians back to the mountains. All this put fear and agitation into the minds of the Austrian and German Princes, which remained even after the Treaty of Campo Formio in October 1797.

Franz Anton felt compelled to remain in Salzburg. But Salzburg, although it supported an orchestra, was averse to encouraging dramatic art, so there was little or no work for the company. Soon, another blow struck the troubled Weber family;

the long-suffering Genofeva died of tuberculosis in March 1798. This tragedy deeply affected young Carl Maria, who had dearly loved his mother. About this time, Franz Anton, still harbouring thoughts of his son as a *Wunderkind*, was successful in placing him in a training school for young choristers under the directorship of the ageing Michael Haydn. No doubt at the insistence of the father, Haydn was persuaded to give the 11-year-old a grounding in composition. But Haydn was rather dry and academic in his approach, completely lacking the enthusiasm of Weber's previous teacher, Heuschkel. Later, he said that he 'had learned little under great stress' from Haydn. Nevertheless, it was while studying with him that Weber composed his first work, a set of six Fughettas for piano solo, dated 1 September 1798. Franz Anton was so delighted with these that he had them printed in the following year. None of the pieces are more than a few bars long, and they're really little more than exercises in composition. They received, however, a generous reception from Johann Rochlitz, the most influential music critic of the day. 'That a young artist like this composer in his eleventh year can compose fugues, and such good ones, is an excellent and unusually promising rarity.' What Rochlitz didn't know was that Franz Anton had boastfully given his son's age as 11 when, in fact, he was 12. Later, Weber was to re-use some of the ideas from these Fughettas in two of his mature works – the opera *Peter Schmoll* and the *Dresden* Mass in E flat major.

At the end of 1798, a reconstituted Weber company travelled on to Munich. This time, Franz Anton's sister, Adelheid, now 69, declined to accompany them. Although the supervision of Weber's daily life now became more erratic than it had ever been, his father realised how important it was that his young son should have regular music lessons. However, his hope of securing the services of the great theorist Joseph Grätz came to nothing, probably because Grätz had understandable doubts as to whether he would ever get paid. Instead, his ex-pupil, Johann Kalcher, a good teacher, agreed to give Weber lessons in composition and piano-playing. Also, the tenor Johann Evangelist Wallishauser, better known as 'Valesi', who had in his younger days been one of the greatest singers in Germany, agreed to give him vocal training. One of Franz Anton's few maxims was that: 'Nobody can write well for the voice, or compose a good opera, without being able to sing decently himself.' For these two teachers Weber always maintained great affection. During this period of intensive study, a time in which, as Max Maria tells us, the boy's mind and body were both overtaxed, Weber was forced to compose a considerable amount of music, including his first opera, *Die Macht der Liebe und des Weins*. Franz Anton, ever keen to cash in on his precocious son, tried to have it published, but without success.

Alois Senefelder, who
invented lithography.

At this time there arrived in Munich a young man with whom
Franz Anton had been previously acquainted in Nuremberg. His
name was Alois Senefelder. Nearly 28, his life had been almost as
eventful as the Webers'. Earmarked for the law, his father's death
had put an end to his studies, and he reverted to the family
business of strolling player, even writing music for his travelling
company. In succession he was artist, soldier and 'half-starved
author', as Max Maria puts it. Although the plays he wrote were
not without merit, Senefelder was unable to interest any publisher
in his work. It was then that he hit on the idea of publishing them
himself, though, as he hadn't the money to buy the necessary
materials, he looked instead for a cheaper method. At first the
results were indifferent, as he had to etch his text onto a copper
plate, which entailed writing backwards. Then, as Senefelder
himself relates, 'my attention was accidentally drawn to a fine
piece of Kellheim stone, which I had purchased for the purpose of
grinding my colours.' By a process of trial and error over a number
of years Senefelder sought a satisfactory way of transferring
lettering to the stone. It was not until 1798, however, that he hit

15

upon the method of relief printing on stone, which we now know as lithography.

Naturally, Franz Anton was overjoyed to renew his friendship with Senefelder, for he saw an opportunity of having his son's works published. Senefelder agreed to take on the young composer as his apprentice and there is little doubt that Weber, ready, as he himself says 'to adopt anything that is new and attracts attention', benefited from working with Senefelder's new invention. However, Weber's later claim that he had 'devised a better method' than Senefelder's might well have been wishful thinking.

At this point, there occurred one of those strokes of misfortune – the work of his 'evil star' as Weber later came to call it – that were to dog him periodically. According to Max Maria 'an inexplicable fire broke out in Kalcher's house where the boy's compositions had been carefully laid aside by his master in a certain cabinet.' Extraordinarily, though the cabinet was completely destroyed, scarcely any other object in the room was touched. The works lost in the fire included his early opera, and Six Variations on an Original Theme for piano. Fortunately, a print had already been

The fascination of fortune-telling.

La diseuse de Bonne Aventure.

16

made of this latter work, which was dedicated in glowing terms to Kalcher, and had drawn another positive response from the critic Rochlitz. Weber, who had inherited from his mother something of a superstitious nature, was stunned by what had happened. All through his life Weber was to be influenced by the thought that one's destiny was directed by supernatural powers. He took this calamity as a warning for him not to continue his musical studies. What excited him now was the wish to exploit Senefelder's invention. But Senefelder had grown jealous of his apprentice's enthusiastic involvement with lithography, no doubt sensing a future rival. The two parties fell out. Ironically, a few months after this – in September 1799, Senefelder, with the Bavarian composer Franz Gleissner, went into partnership with the music publishing house of André in Offenbach, where a lithographic press was established at the beginning of 1800.

Franz Anton and his son went on to Freiberg, initially with the idea of setting up a lithographic business of their own. It was a good place to choose: not only were all the necessary materials to hand, but Freiberg was a lively town, both scientifically and artistically. However, it was to be a short-lived venture. Weber writes in his autobiographical sketch: 'The scale of the enterprise and the purely mechanical, soul destroying work involved soon caused me to abandon the scheme and I returned with redoubled enthusiasm to composition.'

Before leaving the saga of Weber's preoccupation with lithography, it might be revealing to quote a letter the young composer wrote, probably under the supervision of his father, to Artaria of Vienna on 9 October 1800:

I believe that I shall not make your celebrated firm, as music and print sellers, an unwelcome offer and proposal, if I submit for your acceptance the hereafter described *arcanum*. This is an apparatus highly to be recommended, on account of the rapidity with which it works, combined with a small outlay, and which shall become your sole property on the subjoined conditions.

1. I can engrave music on stone in a manner not to be surpassed by the finest English engraving, which the accompanying specimen testifies.
2. A workman in winter is able to complete two or three plates, and in the long summer days, three or four.
3. A plate of this kind can be used afresh thirty times, that is, polished up.
4. Two men can in one week print off as many thousand sheets as can be printed with ordinary type.
5. The whole stock of the machinery does not exceed one hundred thaler.

I await your reply to the enclosed address.

Further, of the musical works I completed while studying under Michael Haydn, I can offer you: Three Easy Trios for violin, viola and violoncello, for dilettanti; Six Variations for the pianoforte; Six ditto; Three ditto, pianoforte sonatas; Six ditto, Variations on the song 'Liebe Augustin'.

I ask six copies of each work and a moderate sum, which I leave you to propose with your usual fairness. In the expectation of a favourable answer on both points, I am, etc.

Weber received no reply from Artaria, who wouldn't have known about Senefelder's lithographic process until the end of 1801 at the earliest, when he and his friend Gleissner introduced it to Vienna. Artaria probably considered Weber's idea wildly fanciful.

In the summer of 1802, after Weber had returned from successful concerts in Erfurt, Gotha and Leipzig, Carl von Steinsberg, the manager of the theatre in Carlsbad, entrusted him with a libretto which he had written called *Das stumme Waldmädchen*. Although Weber had to contend with writing an opera featuring a dumb heroine, he set to work immediately, and finished the second act in ten days. He said at a later date that he had been determined to emulate the feats of other composers!

The first performance of *Das Waldmädchen* (as this opera was called) was given by Steinsberg's company in Freiberg's prestigious Buttermarket Theatre, on 24 November 1800. It had a lukewarm reception, though the music critic, not unkindly, referred to it as 'a mere blossom of genius, which promises better and riper fruit.' Franz Anton interpreted the article as a snub and, replying with an article in his son's name, angrily questioned the competence of the conductor, Siegert. He, in turn, rounded on the composer. The acrimonious and public wrangle continued till January, with little credit to anyone except perhaps Weber himself, who is said to have approached Siegert with a view to reconciliation.

Unfortunately, the score is now lost except for two fragments: perhaps Weber himself destroyed it – he once said that 'Puppies and first operas should be drowned.' In his autobiography he notes that '. . . it was later given further afield than I would have wished, (14 performances in Vienna, translated into Czech for Prague, and successful in St Petersburg) since it is a very immature work with not more than occasional glimpses of inventiveness.'

Nevertheless, Weber thought highly enough of some of the music to re-use it in his later opera *Silvana*.

Chapter 3

Peter Schmoll and Other Works

Following the failure of *Das Waldmädchen* in Freiberg, little is known of Weber's movements for a time. We know that from 24 April to 17 May 1801 he was in Chemnitz (now Karl-Marx Stadt), as there exist letters written by Franz Anton from there. Perhaps, as *Das Waldmädchen* was given in Chemnitz on 5 December 1800, it is possible that Weber and his father made this town their base right through the early months of 1801. By November, however, having visited Munich on the way, they arrived in Salzburg. Though the French, under Moreau, had barely left the city, and confusion was rife, Weber was fortunate in being able to study again with Michael Haydn. Under his watchful eye, this was quite a productive period for the young composer, who remained in Salzburg with his father till the summer of 1802. Here Weber composed his third opera *Peter Schmoll und seine Nachbarn* which was, declared Haydn, 'composed according to the true rules of counterpoint, with much fire and delicacy, and appropriately to the text.' The text was based on a popular romantic novel by Carl Gottlob Cramer, published in 1798/9. The libretto of the opera (by Joseph Türke) has been lost, and indeed, the book itself is a rarity. Jähns, who was to do for Weber what Köchel did for Mozart, could not find a copy at the time he compiled his catalogue, though eventually he acquired one which is now in the Weber collection (Weberiana – German State Library, Berlin). It is not surprising that Weber should have taken to this novel as the basis for an opera, even if his father initially gave him the idea. His highly impressionable and volatile nature would have relished this complicated story of émigrés who had fled the French Revolution and were forming themselves into discontented groups on the German side of the frontier. It struck a note that was only too familiar at the time. Also, it reflected the personal situation of the Webers, a fact which cannot have been lost on the young composer. On the other hand, it is a story full of the new-found affinity with nature, then prevalent in Europe.

The opera is in the form of a *Singspiel* and consists of 20 numbers. Even if the music is Mozartian in style with some near references to tunes from *The Magic Flute*, the score has undoubtedly a charm and freshness of its own. The real achievement for the 15-year-old composer lies in the innate feeling he has for orchestral colour. He writes for unusual and original combinations of instruments (such as two recorders and two bassett horns in No. 14 – The Terzetto), which, while imaginative, are perfectly in keeping with the sung text. There are also glimpses to be seen of the more mature composer. If Weber's ability to instil life into the near cardboard figures of Cramer's novel is only spasmodically achieved (one cannot expect profound character insight from such a young composer), this opera nevertheless shows a marked step forward in self-assurance.

The opera, though completed in 1802, was not performed until the following year. This was in Augsburg, where Weber's brother Edmund, who had left the family entourage in 1798, was installed as conductor of the theatre orchestra in the employ of the wealthy and kindly Prince-Bishop Clemens Wenzeslaus. According to Max Maria the première probably took place in March 1803 though 'no record of success, triumphant or otherwise, is anywhere to be found.' Weber, writing later, confirms the view that it 'had no great success'. Today only the overture is performed in the composer's own revision of 1807.

Apart from *Peter Schmoll*, Weber also revised under Haydn's supervision, the so-called *Jugendmesse*, which he had begun while studying with Kalcher. A fair copy, dated 3 May 1802, disappeared until discovered in the Salzburg Museum in 1925.

In the autumn of 1802 Weber, with his father, returned to the town of his birth, Eutin, travelling through Meiningen, Eisenach, Sondershausen and Brunswick. Once in Eutin, where Franz Anton had some private affairs to settle, Weber came into contact with the poet Johann Heinrich Voss, who supplied him with various verses for songs, though only two of them were by himself. One of these was an exquisite poem by Matthisson called *Die Kerze*, which Weber set while in Hamburg that October. Thus started Weber's lifelong interest in *Lieder*. He was to write about 90 solo songs, some of them comparing well with the best of Schubert. Sadly, they are seldom performed today. Also, probably while in Hamburg, Weber wrote Six Écossaises for piano solo inscribed 'To the fair sex of Hamburg', indicating that his development wasn't exclusively musical.

Returning to Augsburg in December, Weber produced further vocal works: a three-part vocal canon *Mädchen, ach meide Männerschmeichelei'n* (which Mahler was to use later for his

An evening of chamber music.

completion of Weber's *Die drei Pintos*) and other pieces for various combinations of voices.

In the closing weeks of 1802 Weber, along with his father and brother Edmund, was often invited by Prince-Bishop Wenzeslaus to his palace in Augsburg, to make music. Wenzeslaus loved music and Max Maria relates that:

> . . . many a pleasant evening passed in concerted performances, wherein Edmund led on the violin; the Bishop himself, and the son of his court physician, Ahorner, took the viola or flute; Franz Anton flourished on the violoncello or bass, and Carl Maria played the piano or sang.

Chapter 4

Vienna 1803

Peter Schmoll had not excited any interest and Franz Anton was impatient to be on the move again. This time the city chosen was Vienna, where Haydn and Beethoven were still firmly enthroned. Probably Weber himself felt that a period of further study was needed to iron out the deficiencies in his compositional technique particularly with regard to opera. It seems as though

Vienna, c. 1800.

Joseph Haydn was the teacher they initially had in mind, for Max Maria records that when Weber arrived in Vienna he had with him a recommendation from Joseph Haydn's brother, Michael. This was late in the summer of 1803. But Weber's hopes were quickly dashed: Haydn was now 71 and slowly retiring from the outside world.

Only a year before, however, there had returned to Vienna from a series of travels lasting no less than 20 years, a figure who had already excited the musical firmament with his exotic and flamboyant style of living – the composer and pedagogue Abbé Georg Josef Vogler. Born in 1749, he was a precocious child, self-taught on the violin and on a number of other instruments including the organ. He studied under Mozart's revered teacher Padre Martini, but rebelled at the constant discipline that Martini demanded; so much so that the master complained of his pupil's lack of aptitude and perseverance. In fact, there was more than a little similarity between the characters of Vogler and Franz Anton. They both loved a wandering, exuberant lifestyle, and were vain and eccentric by nature. Weber probably came to see a certain kinship between his father, whom he dearly loved, and the colourful Vogler. Apart from this affinity of nature, the reason for Franz Anton favouring Vogler for his son's new teacher would almost certainly have been his extravagant reputation, which he had acquired with the successes of his elaborate compositions and concert tours around the courts of Europe.

Many years later the poet Robert Browning, who was born in 1814, just two years before Vogler died, wrote a long euphoric poem bearing his name. On the other hand, the nineteenth-century German scholar Otto Jahn considered Vogler as one of those musical philosophers who disguise their lack of solid musical schooling in a vast ostentation of general culture. However, Weber himself, writing in 1810, had nothing but adulation for his teacher and even began work on a full-scale biography of Vogler in the same year.

Weber's initial contact with his teacher-to-be is described vividly by Max Maria:

In the house of Count Firmian young Carl Maria made the acquaintance of Johann Baptist Gänsbacher, a young officer, who had lately retired from the service with a golden medal, in order to turn his ardent passion for music to account, by studying under the Abbé Vogler. Gänsbacher was a fine powerful broad-shouldered fellow who, in addition to his adored art, loved wine, women and rifle-shooting, of which he was a master. His free, jovial nature made a striking impression on the lad who quickly felt the influence of a companion older than himself by eight years and soon learned to love him with an ardent and enduring

Abbé Georg Josef Vogler, composer and pedagogue.

friendship. Very speedily he shared in all his new friend's youthful follies, joys, sorrows, purposes and aspirations. The affection was reciprocal: and young Gänsbacher's first service to Weber was rendered in obtaining for him a hearing with the Abbé Vogler. The boy's own talent did the rest.

Weber quickly came under the spell of his new master, whose mystical airs lent profundity to his conversation even if it was short on factual knowledge.

Today, Vogler's music is almost forgotten. Although it shows remarkable facility (and is not without melodic grace and even more harmonic interest), it lacks contrast and real direction. He also initiated a new theoretical system which impressed Weber, as can be seen from the following letter written to a flautist friend, Ignaz Susann in October 1803:

I have had the joy of getting to know Abbé Vogler, who is my best friend and with whom I am now studying his magnificent system. Every day I am with him for four or five hours. Imagine my happiness when I was with him in the evening a few days ago (you are to understand that he is writing an opera for the *Theater an der Wien* of which NOT A SOUL has seen or heard anything because he composes entirely in the night) and all at once he runs out into the third room, locks the door, closes the shutters, and acts so busily that I haven't an idea what it all means. At last he produces a stack of music, sits down at the piano, and plays to me – after I take an oath of solemn silence – the overture and other pieces from his opera. It is really heavenly music and then – what do you suppose? – he gives me his own score of the overture written in his very own hand in order that, little by little, I can work out the piano version of the whole opera. Now I sit over it and study and rejoice like the very devil for happiness.

Vogler's secret opera, for which Weber was so diligently preparing a vocal score, was called *Samori*. No doubt, the enormous amount of hard work that Vogler's enthusiastic pupil had to put in constituted payment for the lessons that he received. These were hard, grinding lessons, in which the young composer had to curtail his own creative inventiveness in exchange for sheer drudgery. Vogler made Weber persevere as he himself presumably never did under Martini. Weber's own motto, particularly in the early years of his life – *'Beharrlichkeit führt zum Ziel'* ('perseverance achieves its object') – took on a new meaning.

Weber composed little at this time and what he did manage to write did not show much, if any, of Vogler's influence, least of all his system. However, in reverence to his master Weber composed two sets of variations; Eight Variations for piano on the *Air de Ballet* from Vogler's earlier opera *Castore e Polluce*; and Six

Variations for piano, with optional violin and cello accompaniment, on an aria from *Samori*.

Meanwhile, during all this industry on Weber's part, Franz Anton took himself off to Salzburg and Augsburg on business. For the first time Weber was left to his own devices, which, happening as it did in the metropolis of Vienna, with all its giddy distractions, was a considerable temptation for the susceptible young 17-year-old. With the ebullient and dissolute Gänsbacher, Weber was introduced into the fun-loving society of the city, which soon took to the lean, handsome and charming composer, who also sang so beautifully while accompanying himself with great delicacy on the guitar.

In April 1804 we find Weber writing again to Susann:

It was no small thing for a creative soul to sit in such productive surroundings for nine months and not write a note; but it was my firm intention to listen, learn and collect for a long while before I wrote anything again.

Certainly this prolonged period of concentrated study with Vogler was just what Weber needed to consolidate his technique. On the other hand, Vogler must have been impressed by Weber's intimate knowledge of stagecraft. This undoubtedly had a bearing on Vogler's decision to recommend Weber for the post of *Kapellmeister*, along with Gänsbacher, when Johann Rhode, Director of the theatre at Breslau, wrote requesting him to put forward some names. Gänsbacher turned down the nomination. Weber accepted, little knowing what he was letting himself in for. On 8 May 1804, the appointment was confirmed. Max Maria reveals that:

It was a hard struggle for the lad to quit Vienna and its pleasures. The separation from Vogler, Gänsbacher and his many friends cost him dear – still dearer the necessity of tearing himself away from an attachment formed with a lady of rank, who, older than the stripling, seems to have loved him ardently. The struggle was indeed a hard one. But gratified ambition, the allurement of a comparatively independent position, the hope of earning a provision for the old spendthrift, Franz Anton, were powerful motives for his decision to accept the offer.

After rejoining his father in Salzburg, Weber, by way of Augsburg and Carlsbad arrived in Breslau on 11 June 1804.

In Salzburg Weber had penned his first love song, which was inspired, so we are told, by the Viennese love affair already alluded to – it was called 'Wiedersehen'.

Chapter 5

Breslau and Near Calamity

For one so young to step into the important position of *Kapellmeister* in an influential town like Breslau, was a feat bound to raise a few eyebrows, as well as the blood pressure of those local candidates who had been eyeing the job for themselves. Joseph Schnabel, the versatile and talented leader of the orchestra, was just such a person. He had already begun directing the performances before Weber arrived on the scene. 37 years old, he was more than twice the age of Weber. He promptly resigned,

Breslau.

but, by taking on other musical posts in the town that were quickly offered him, he remained close by to make Weber's life in Breslau that much more difficult. Then there were the numerous Prussian nobility, who could hardly believe their eyes when they saw the aristocratic 'von' that Franz Anton had so unashamedly inserted into the Weber name. Such was the prejudice of the time that the nobility took it ill that a youth of title should degrade himself by becoming a mere musician, whilst on the other hand, the lower classes grew suspicious of him because of his title.

Nevertheless, the young and highly recommended new *Kapellmeister* was received with kindness and courtesy by the management of the theatre. The orchestra had been freshly recruited, and it contained some of the best instrumentalists of the day. However, since they were badly paid, their commitment was questionable; if they could find more lucrative engagements they would be sure to leave.

Weber himself was not badly paid and, if his father hadn't run up debts in a business enterprise, would have been financially secure.

On arriving in Breslau, Weber embarked on a number of innovations to the whole organisation of opera with an assurance and vigour that was no doubt part instinct and part derived from the cumulative experience he had gained over the years with his father's theatrical company. He busied himself first with the rearrangement of the players' seating in the orchestra. Tradition had it that the wind should sit in front, with the strings at the rear. Weber insisted that the first violins, oboes, horns, one cello and one bass should be placed on the right; the second violins, clarinets and bassoons were to be on the left, with the violas behind. Then, right at the back he put the trumpets and drums. This is similar to the seating arrangement we have today, but the Breslau audiences, who were used to the sound of brass (they boasted a military establishment in the town), were not impressed. They were used to the massive array of wind instruments in front (woodwind players were in those days nearly as numerous as the strings), which projected a blanket of sound that largely stifled the strings. Weber, quite understandably, wanted to obtain a finer and more subtle balance from his orchestral forces. This rearrangement initiated a storm of protest, which found further outlet when Weber began to dismiss artists who were past their prime, or whose talent was obviously meagre. In any case, he had upset the singers by giving more attention to the orchestra than to them.

Apart from this, Weber, far from leaving behind all the wild and dissolute living of his Viennese days, directed what spare energy he had after his work in Breslau to further riotous living

27

and passionate love affairs. There is no doubt that Weber was extremely attractive to women. Max Maria tells us:

Many a female heart, both within the theatre and without, was allured by the sweet smile and seductive manners of the pale, slender, languishing, but passionately ardent young conductor.

One of Weber's more indiscreet affairs became the subject of gossip in the town and probably caused particular consternation for the management of the theatre as it involved a prima donna in the company by the name of Diezel. However, Johann Rhode, the director, steadfastly supported the young conductor.

Another friend he had in Breslau, who he quickly got to know on his arrival, was Friedrich Wilhelm Berner, the principal clarinettist in the theatre orchestra. He was also an excellent

Weber, painted by Caroline Bardua.

pianist, and, in both these spheres, Weber held him in highest regard. Although later in life Berner became famous for his didactic writings, he also composed a number of works for the clarinet, and songs for voices and instruments which were very popular at the time. It is very probable that prior to Weber's close association with the clarinettist Heinrich Bärmann, which wasn't to commence until some six years later, Berner was to exercise a significant influence on Weber, not only as a composer but also as an individual. Max Maria has this to say about Berner:

He was about six years Weber's senior, and Weber found in him a nature congenial to his own – generous, ebullient, animated, almost reckless in its wild love of life and life's enjoyments. Both the young men were ardent worshippers of their art, both eager in the pursuit of pleasure. But Berner, despite his joviality, was a hard-working and highly-educated artist; and his influence upon the budding genius he took to his bosom, with as much admiration as love, was in many respects a powerful one. Carl Maria recognised his superior knowledge, and profited by his advice in composition.

Another of Weber's sweeping innovations at the theatre – and one which many people in Breslau did not take to kindly – was a drastic change in repertoire. Instead of continuing with operas that were inferior, but made good box-office sense, he introduced new works including *La Clemenza di Tito* (which the critics acclaimed), *Don Giovanni* and a version of *Così fan Tutte* with additional text by Rhode. Mozart was still far from being accepted

Announcement of the first performance of *Don Giovanni*.

everywhere, and Rhode, who had dramatic ambitions himself, naturally hoped to enhance his own reputation with these adaptations. To further this end, he began to interest Weber in a libretto he had previously published called *Rübezahl*, which was based on an old Silesian folk-tale. Only three numbers survive in Weber's setting, and as he later referred to them as a fragment, he probably composed little more. But he did complete the overture, which, in 1811, he reworked as *Der Beherrscher der Geister*, and in which guise it is still performed today.

Connected with the original overture hangs a real-life drama that could, with no exaggeration, have fundamentally altered the whole course of Romantic opera in Germany. Weber asked his friend Berner to come to his house one evening, and go through with him the *Rübezahl* music, including the overture. Max Maria vividly unfolds the events that followed:

A light at Weber's window showed that he was within. Berner mounted the step, knocked at the door – no answer; again – no note of friendly welcome. At last, he pushed open the door and entered. The lamp was on the table – the piano open – but where was Carl Maria? By the sofa Berner stumbled. What was it? He had fallen upon the lifeless body of his friend; by his side a broken bottle, emitting a strong odour. Berner raised up the apparent corpse in his arms, and shouted for help.

Franz Anton hurried in from another room, alarmed. With a glance, he discovered that the bottle had contained a deadly acid used in his engraving. His boy was poisoned. Doctors were called in: and, with difficulty, the unhappy youth was brought back to life. But his mouth and windpipe were frightfully burned – his voice was gone. For weeks Weber lay between life and death. At last came the merest whisper of a voice, the full force of which was never to return. The invalid could now explain that, shivering with cold from prolonged work, he had stretched out his hand for a flask of wine which he knew was on the table, and had seized the bottle of nitric acid instead.

Weber was consequently out of action for two months and his beautiful singing voice never returned.

In the meantime, Weber's enemies, including the hostile Schnabel, took advantage of his absence from the theatre and cancelled his reforms. With his authority apparently undermined, Weber threw up his arms in disgust and, in spite of entreaties from Rhode and his friends to stay on, resigned.

Harassed by his creditors, and hampered by his father, who was now an invalid, Weber resorted to the stock family reaction to problems of this kind: he declared his intention to go into the wide world as a 'tramping musical pedlar'.

Fortunately, at this point, Weber's friend Berner was once again his unwitting saviour. Berner had been in the generous habit of passing on some of his pupils to Weber. One of these was Fräulein von Belonde, maid of honour to the Duchess of Württemberg. The Duchess's husband, Duke Eugen of Württemberg, had been the ruler of Carlsruhe, a small town in Upper Silesia some 40 miles from Breslau, since 1793.

In the Duke's early youth he had been a rake – 'a passionate admirer of female beauty' as Max Maria discreetly puts it. Later he became interested in the occult, until finally music became his abiding passion. As Max Maria colourfully describes:

When the domain of Carlsruhe fell into his possession by the extinction of another branch of the Württemberg family, he not only reconstructed his palace and made of the secluded residence a brilliant little court where powdered and pigtailed courtiers with cocked-hats and swords wandered hand-in-hand with lofty-wigged and high-heeled beauties, but he built a magnificent theatre which many a capital might have envied, and installed a little dramatic and operatic world around him.

Fräulein von Belonde was much taken with her pale and amiable piano teacher whose ability at improvisation she particularly admired. She was also touched by the sad plight he was in and, knowing that the Duke had been impressed when he had seen him conduct in Breslau, urged Weber to appeal direct to the Duke for his patronage. This Weber did, although his passport was already in his pocket in readiness to begin his travels. Weber's petition, no doubt largely dictated by Franz Anton, was couched in a boastful manner with much false information about the family's noble lineage. In response, the Duke, while offering Weber the honorary office of Musical Director, made it clear that it was on account of his own distinguished talent alone, and 'in no manner whatever on account of his family'. The snub aside, the titular position offered no real help to Weber, who was now in desperate straits. Travel was out of the question. On the political front, the French victories in Austria and Southern Germany posed a real threat to Breslau itself. Fräulein von Belonde, realising how difficult the situation was for Weber, herself appealed to the Duke to offer him asylum. In the circumstances, the Duke acceded to this request, later including Franz Anton and Aunt Adelheid, who had fled in alarm from the advancing French armies.

Chapter 6

A Golden Dream

Apart from the *Rübezahl* fragments, Weber composed very little during the two years he was in Breslau. Some indication of the way his imagination was working – towards the exotic and oriental – is apparent in two pieces he did write at this time. One was the *Romanza Siciliana* for flute and orchestra, which is supposed to

Duke Eugen Friedrich
Heinrich of Württemberg
in cavalry dress.

have been based on 'original Saracen–Sicilian motives', and the other, an *Overtura Chinesa*, no longer extant, which he remodelled later into an overture for Schiller's German adaptation of Gozzi's fable *Turandot* (the source also of Puccini's *Turandot*).

In his new surroundings at the Duke's beautiful estate of Carlsruhe, Weber was able to revitalise both his mind and body. In a landscape not unlike that of his native Eutin, he was soon able to relax and turn his thoughts once more to composition. Few things were expected of him, and none demanded, for he was not on the Duke's payroll. Max Maria gives a cosy account of Weber's lifestyle:

His breakfast was brought him by the ducal lackeys; but at dinner he was an expected and ever-welcome guest at the palace. Theatrical rehearsals and performances occupied much of his time. But the greatest charm of this delightful little court lay in the evenings, passed in the more select family circle, when music, wit, female fascination, amiability, and fine feeling all combined under the guidance of that clever, excellent, friendly worshipper-of-art-and-artist's-talent, the Duke Eugen.

Amongst the first compositions to result from Weber's blissful new way of life was a short flourish or fanfare for 20 trumpets. Exactly why he composed this is not known; the most likely explanation is that it was required for some special occasion at the palace. No doubt in appreciation of Fräulein von Belonde's efforts on his behalf, Weber composed a song for her called 'Ich denke dein', which in places is quite Schubertian. He also wrote Six Variations for viola based on an Austrian tune, which was subsequently discovered by Jähns in Stuttgart.

Weber, naturally, felt tremendously indebted to the Duke for his timely generosity, and composed his only two symphonies in honour of him. Of the two, the first certainly deserves to be more frequently performed. The first movement, for all its formal deficiencies, has an infectiously joyous sweep to it, and Weber later referred to it as 'a wild fantasy movement, perhaps in Overture style, in disjointed sections'. But the Minuet was the movement Weber was most pleased with. A real Scherzo in the Beethovian sense, it is strongly rhythmical with a touch of impish humour. The Finale is a busy, thrusting movement interlaced with carefree tunes.

The second symphony is most noteworthy for its slow movement, which is very imaginative in its orchestral colouring. Weber, in one place, uses the darker-hued instruments, the violas, against a background of wind chords, to a wholly original tonal structure.

Another work written during Weber's temporary residence at

the ducal palace was the Concertino for horn and orchestra, composed expressly for Dantrevaux, a famous horn player, then a member of the orchestra. In addition, there was a virtuoso piece for solo piano – Seven Variations on 'Vien qua, Dorina bella' – an air by the prolific Italian opera composer, Francesco Bianchi.

Weber's *sojourn* in Carlsruhe, though idyllic by all accounts – he was to refer to it later as 'a golden dream' – was comparatively short-lived. The Prussian forces had been relentlessly pushed back by the invading French, who were now in Berlin and Warsaw. To make matters worse:

. . . in and around Carlsruhe lay the Württemberg troops, then in alliance with the French. They were commanded by the vicious General Vandamme, who took pleasure and pride in urging his German troops to exceed the pitch of unbridled licentiousness and savage barbarity of the French. Thus, he could make them even more abhorrent to their own countrymen than the foreigner.

The Duke Eugen, who was now serving in the Prussian army as a general, feared an attack on his estate, not only from the French, but from the marauding German troops too. Though, in fact, the Duke's property was respected by the marauders, Weber had to witness, day after day, round the palace, crowds of unhappy wretches from the vicinity, mourning their murdered relatives and weeping over the loss of all their possessions.

Some writers have assumed that Weber's departure in February 1807 from Carlsruhe was directly due to the disbandment of the resident ensemble, but as Warrack convincingly explains in his book, this was not the case. He asserts that 'it continued until 1809 (a musician named Weber, presumably Franz Anton, is recorded as receiving a lodging allowance in 1808)'. However, Warrack concludes that Weber's departure remains obscure. This may be so, but the present writer puts forward the suggestion that Weber, sickened by the surrounding misery, felt impelled to get away. The sharp contrast to the earlier idyllic days on the estate must have not only caused him worry and frustration, but seemed nonsensical to Weber, who abhorred anything to do with war and aggressors.

The Duke was again in a position to help him. Though heavily involved in the war, he found time to communicate with his brothers, Friedrich 1, King of Württemberg, and the profligate Duke Ludwig. As it happened, Duke Ludwig was in need of a private secretary, and Weber was accepted on the strong recommendation of Duke Eugen. Leaving his father and aunt behind, he left Carlsruhe on 23 February 1807. However, far from going straight to Stuttgart where Duke Ludwig resided, and taking up his new employment, he spent the next five months on the road, first travelling to Breslau to collect some papers. Once here, he took the opportunity to contact some of his old friends. Having now recovered some of his former equanimity, a few carefree days followed, which were brought to a sudden halt when he was recognised by a creditor, and had to leave 'furtively at early dawn'.

Before arriving in Stuttgart on 17 July, Weber fitted in a mini-concert tour of towns round Nuremberg, probably with the clarinettist and violinist Gottfried Backofen, who had been a member of the municipal orchestra in Nuremberg since 1803.

Chapter 7

A Period of Licentiousness and Misadventure at a Dissolute Court

Weber was unsuited in every way for the job of private secretary to Duke Ludwig, and he can't have had the remotest idea what was expected of him. In fact, his duties were wide-ranging, as Benedict makes clear:

Poor Weber had not only to undertake the private correspondence of the Duke, to regulate as controller the expenses of the household, manage the privy purse and keep the books of receipts and disbursements, but to act as mediator with the King when the affairs of the Duke were in a desperate plight.

And as the Duke's affairs were indeed often in a desperate plight, Weber, who invariably acted as 'go-between', had to suffer the full brunt of the King's anger which was turned on him with ever-increasing venom.

The King loathed Weber even more than he did his spendthrift brother. Weber, for his part, had nothing but hatred for the King, whose wild excesses he witnessed daily, and who treated him with contempt and scorn. Often, on the occasions when Weber had to seek further funds for the Duke, the King, after letting him wait for hours in an antechamber, would abruptly dismiss him, unheard.

On one such occasion, when Weber was irritated beyond words, he had the chance to play a reckless prank on the King. Smarting under the injustice of the King's behaviour, Weber, after leaving the King's private apartment, suddenly came across an old woman in the passageway. She asked where she could find the room of the court washerwoman and Weber pointed to the door he had just left. On entering, the old woman was violently assailed by the King who had a horror of old women. Being terrified, she blurted out that a young gentleman had just shown her where to find the 'royal washerwoman'. Livid with rage, and guessing the culprit, the monarch immediately dispatched an officer to arrest the unfortunate Weber and lock him up.

For a whole day he languished in the royal prison, but the time was put to good use. The room contained a dilapidated piano, which Weber proceeded to tune with an ordinary door key. Here he composed the somewhat embittered song 'Ein steter Kampf ist unser Leben'.

The King was poles apart in character, intellect and culture from his brother, the Duke Eugen. For a start, he was enormously fat and Max Maria tells us: 'his unwieldy corpulence increased so frightfully that, even in 1807 a semi-circular space was cut in his dining tables to permit him to approach near enough to feed himself.'

Apart from his personal appearance, he was also tyrannical and corrupt. When Napoleon had invaded his territory, he shamelessly insinuated himself into the dictator's favour and was rewarded with being pronounced King of the state of Württemberg.

His brother Duke Ludwig was, if anything, an even more unworthy figure, dissolute and widely involved in shadowy intrigues. He did not care for music and only visited the opera so that he could gaze at the women. At least the King, besides hunting, gambling and drinking, enjoyed music. Indeed, he was a great supporter of opera in Stuttgart, where an ecstatic Napoleon is reported to have attended a performance of *Don Giovanni*.

Duties apart, these were not idle days for Weber who, during the two and a half years he was in Stuttgart, composed his opera, *Silvana*, the cantata *Der erste Ton* for reciter and orchestra, 16 songs along with other minor vocal pieces, and nine instrumental works – 31 compositions all told.

Weber also took advantage of the flourishing intellectual life that was prevalent in Stuttgart. Through the director of the royal library, Dr Lehr, a sensitive poet and an amiable man, he was introduced to the world of books. With his guidance 'he derived the most valuable hints for the improvement of his style, his habit of thought and the direction of his critical and philosophical studies'. He read, amongst others, the writings of Kant. Along with this intensive study, Weber had the chance to meet a number of influential poets, playwrights and artists. One such was the sculptor Dannecker, just then occupied with his celebrated *Ariadne*; another was Matthison, the poet of Beethoven's *Adelaide* and the first poet to inspire Weber as a songwriter with his 'Die Kerze'. Weber also met Ludwig Spohr for the first time. He was

37

Portrait of the violinist and composer Ludwig Spohr.

already considered one of the outstanding violinists of his time, and was fast gaining recognition as a composer. Weber played him some extracts from *Rübezahl* which Spohr privately considered 'insignificant and amateurish'. Although the two composers were to remain friends until Weber's death, their regard for each other differed widely – Weber consistently praised Spohr's musicality, but Spohr never held a very high opinion of Weber.

The other composer Weber met in Stuttgart was Franz Danzi, whose influence and friendship he could always count on. It was Danzi who proposed Weber for a select society known as *Faust's Höllenfahrt* (Faust's ride to hell), where each member was assigned a nickname. The unprepossessing title of '*Krautsalat*' (Cabbage salad) was allotted to Weber. On the face of it, the society may seem to have been a flippant affair, but for all the good-natured fun that it generated, it nevertheless gave artists the *camaraderie* and mutual support that they sorely needed during such an unstable period.

38

Franz Danzi, born in 1763, was considerably older than Weber. He too, had been a pupil of Vogler, and before taking on the new appointment of court conductor at Stuttgart in 1807, he had been involved with the famous orchestra at Mannheim.

Certainly, Danzi was largely responsible for re-directing Weber's mind to composition, and became a steadying influence amidst the many temptations of the dissolute court. Their friendship grew, with Weber developing a respect and affection for the older composer bordering on veneration. On many occasions Danzi, a plump little man, with a round head and sharp, clever, good-tempered eyes, was seen making a joyous country outing in the vicinity of Stuttgart, deep in conversation with the lively youth.

Weber was to repay Danzi's acts of kindness by dedicating a number of works to him including *Der erste Ton*, which signalled a new departure for the young composer. Based on a poem of that name by Rochlitz, the poet and critic who had previously spoken generously about Weber's earliest compositions, it treats the creation of the universe out of chaos, and the whole of nature receiving inspiration through the medium of sound – hence the title, *'The First Sound'*. Although influenced by Haydn's *Creation*, it is really entirely different in concept. Rather than relying on recitative to carry the story along, Weber, in this melodramatic cantata, makes use of declamation by a speaker, sometimes unaccompanied, at other points with rich orchestral colours. Here, in a pioneering work, was Weber reflecting in music the newly developing Romantic movement that was sweeping through Europe.

Der erste Ton was to prove an unusually successful work, being performed quite frequently during Weber's life. It was performed in all the great cities of Germany, generally to considerable critical acclaim, and did far more for Weber's career than any of his other works had done to date.

The only other work that Weber wrote for Danzi during his Stuttgart years was the incidental music for a production of Schiller's drama *Turandot* in September 1809. Schiller had adapted Gozzi's play in the late autumn of 1801 for the German National Theatre in Weimar, being much taken with the oriental and bizarre nature of the work.

Apart from these new compositions, Weber also revised this incidental music for *Turandot (Overtura chinesa)* for the Stuttgart production, adding six further pieces. Only one is not based on the single theme of the overture, and that is No. 3, a March. Instead, this is founded on a tune given in Rousseau's *Dictionnaire de la Musique* (1768), where it is referred to as an *air chinois*. In Weber's own review of a concert for workhouse inmates, which he himself organised and conducted in 1816, he wrote: 'Pipes and drums introduce the strange, bizarre melody, which is then taken up by the whole orchestra and presented in a number of different shapes, figurations and keys.'

When Hindemith, in this century, came to write the second movement of his *Symphonic Metamorphosis* on themes by Weber, where he utilised the March, we would perhaps agree that it was not only the tune that attracted him, but also Weber's clever use of it.

Another member of the 'Faust' society was Franz Karl Hiemer. He was a man of many talents, the sort of person who would appeal to the young Weber: occasional soldier, painter, actor, court official and poet, and currently trying to make his reputation as a dramatist and librettist. Weber, whose choice of librettists was often to prove suspect and ill-considered despite his own literary skill, saw in Hiemer the man to provide him with a libretto. Soon after his arrival in Stuttgart, he had given Hiemer the discarded libretto of *Das Waldmädchen* to work on. But Hiemer, whose lifestyle was even more dissolute than Weber's, was also careless and lazy. The opera *Silvana*, which the work was to become, wasn't completed until February 1810, a good two years later, and even then only after continual proddings from Weber for more of the text.

Weber's life in Stuttgart was strongly influenced by a soprano connected with the theatre called Margarethe Lang. She seems to have won Weber's heart to such an extent that he neglected his duties, and the affair eventually came to the notice of the King. Fräulein Lang also helped to relieve Weber by her extravagances of a fair proportion of his meagre salary, so that he slipped further and further into debt. On a more positive note, she did inspire him to compose *Lieder*, and under her influence Weber produced some of his most charming songs, such as 'Was zieht zu deinem Zauberkreise' of 1809. Besides his mounting debts, other troubles loomed on the horizon with the arrival in April 1809 of his father, Franz Anton. Sporting a 'bass viol and two enormous basket-beds for his two dearly beloved poodles', Max Maria tells us 'he fell, like a chimney-pot in a storm, on his son's head.' With the death of Aunt Adelheid, Franz Anton, now over 75, must have felt the need to be with his son. Unfortunately, although time had dimmed his wits, it hadn't lessened his exasperating habit of interfering with his son's affairs, however well meaning his intentions might have been.

Towards the end of 1809, Weber discovered, to his horror and dismay, that his father had taken some 800 gulden, given to Weber by the Duke to purchase horses in Silesia.

Franz Anton, without a thought, had sent the entire sum to Carlsruhe to pay off his debts. The Duke soon discovered that the money hadn't reached its destination, and Weber, quite openly, confessed to his patron the whole sorry tale. In an attempt to repay the money, Weber tried to borrow the required sum from Höner, the landlord of Schwieberdingen country inn, where he had been a good customer, but he was unsuccessful. Then, out of the blue, Höner changed his mind and sent a thousand gulden. Weber, with relief, repaid the debt, little realising that Höner had an ulterior motive. The landlord, assuming that Weber held some sway with the King – who was known for his practice of selling court positions to handsome young men – took it that Weber would put forward his son. He was of military age, and this would therefore save him from being drafted into the army. Weber remained blissfully unaware of this, having forgotten the monarch's corrupt practice. When Höner's son was called up in January 1810, the disappointed landlord wasted no time in bringing an action against Weber to recover the loan. The matter came before the King who, gleefully seeing his chance of belittling the 'forward young puppy of a secretary', agreed to take action. Max Maria, in writing about the incident, furnishes further details:

A few weeks before this discovery, *Silvana* had been finished. Danzi had obtained the permission of Count Winzingerode, the Director, to prepare the young composer's opera for immediate production. Carl Maria was daily, for many hours at a time, in the theatre making arrangements for the long-desired performance. He was thus employed on the evening of 9 February 1810, when suddenly the orchestra was invaded by a body of officials, who arrested Weber in the name of the King and, without even leaving him time to say a last few words to Danzi, dragged him off to prison. His father, he learned, was under arrest in his own apartment.

Things looked very bad indeed for Weber. For 16 days he was kept under close confinement, not really aware of what he was supposed to have done wrong. Worse, most of his friends deserted him, with the exception of Danzi, who steadfastly proclaimed Weber's innocence. Max Maria writes that 'Danzi alone was true as steel.' One of the accusations was a trumped-up charge concerning valuable articles found in his quarters, which even the King, hostile as he was, didn't believe. The question of embezzlement of the Duke's money no longer arose, since it had been re-paid. The final charge had serious implications though, as it involved the possibility of bribery associated with a deliberate attempt to avoid military service. Suddenly the King, who had been clandestinely behind the practice of selling appointments for years, realised that he had better let the matter drop before too much was uncovered. Banishment from the King's domain was

Travelling by post coach.

just about to be effected, when numerous creditors pounced upon the luckless composer and he was rearrested. However, on condition that Weber paid off his debts by instalments, the King refrained from pressing official charges. Weber was released again, but the matter did not end there. The King gave orders that the Webers, father and son, should be transported immediately over the boundaries of Württemberg, never to return. On the morning of 26 February 1810 they were unceremoniously awakened by a police commissary, ordered to pack their belongings, and put into a carriage which was to take them to the nearest frontier point. All they had between them was 40 gulden, but the police officer who accompanied them was convinced, like many other inhabitants of Stuttgart, of Weber's innocence, and pressed 25 gulden of his own into his hand. He also passed on to Weber several letters of introduction to friends in Mannheim, which the loyal Danzi had given him.

Chapter 8

Weber Emerges as a Writer

There were to be a number of advantages for the Webers in making Mannheim their destination, some foreseen and others that only came about through happy coincidence.

In the first place, Mannheim was still a town of considerable musical importance. Though it no longer enjoyed the reputation of possessing the best opera in Germany (indeed the opera house had been virtually razed to the ground by the French artillery), Napoleon and the revolutionaries had failed to destroy Mannheim's love for the arts and, in particular, music. A new theatre was erected on the same site as the old, and Peter Ritter was installed as conductor. Through a letter of introduction given him by Danzi, Weber got to know this genial musician, who was also steadily making his name as a composer. Amongst Weber's first writings as a critic (he had a natural flair for this and consistently practised into the 1820s) was a notice of one of Ritter's most successful operas *Der Zitherschläger*. The review is dated 1 April and is interesting not so much for its actual content, but for the way Weber was quite prepared to disregard his personal safety. The political situation was still tense, but he says quite openly:

In fact our warmest thanks are due to Herr Ritter and his librettist for an original German opera which can stand comparison with any French opera of the same kind.

Not only is this a courageous statement, but it also gives us the first concrete evidence of Weber's life-long dream of establishing a truly national German school of opera.

Through another of Danzi's letters of introduction Weber got to know Gottfried Weber. This Weber, who shared no ancestral connection with the young composer, was already, at the age of 31, chief of the revenue department in Mannheim; a man of exceptional ability, who combined tact, industry and energy. He was also a very talented musician, having mastered at an early age

43

An evening of chamber music.

a number of instruments, including the organ, cello and flute.

In the previous year (1809), a society called the Carl-Stephanie Museum had been formed in Mannheim to put on amateur concerts of a high artistic standard. Gottfried Weber was appointed conductor of both the orchestra and chorus. Only a few weeks before the Webers' arrival, he had married Augusta von Dusch, a charming and beautiful woman with a fine soprano voice. The domestic arrangements were such that Gottfried's own father, who was of a similar age to Franz Anton, was able to offer the old man lodging in his house, thus taking a great weight off Weber's mind. Gottfried and the young composer got on well together from the first and soon became firm friends.

With his father cared for, Weber moved on to Heidelberg with Gottfried to visit Alexander von Dusch, Augusta's brother, who was an enthusiastic amateur cellist. Almost immediately, a similar close bond developed between Weber and Dusch, who, still a student at the university, carried Weber off triumphantly into the local musical world. He fixed a meeting for Weber with the Musical Director and Organist Friedrich Joseph Hoffmann, who held the post of an academic *Kapellmeister* to the university. Whilst Hoffmann tried to organise a concert for Weber, Weber himself was arranging 'a serenade of students in honour of the most admired *belles* of the ball-room', which proved a great success. Unfortunately, on a later occasion, some of these very students got out of hand, and a quarrel developed into a riot. Military troops had to be dispatched to Heidelberg to quell the uproar. As a consequence of this, the concert that Hoffmann had so painstakingly secured for Weber had to be cancelled.

Weber returned to Mannheim, where he had some consolation in the fact that Gottfried had in the meantime arranged a concert to take place on 9 March. It was a success artistically, but not financially, netting the composer only 13 gulden. With the Stuttgart debts demanding attention, Weber sought to arrange a further concert which, after some problems, took place on 2 April, and was much more successful financially. It included a repeat performance of the First Symphony and also the première of *Der erste Ton*. The famous tragic actor Ferdinand Esslair declaimed the verses of Rochlitz's poem with such power and inspiration that the audience burst into a tumult of applause before the final chorus. Max Maria relates that: 'It was a proud moment in the young composer's life. The musician, the lover of art and the critic, were all unanimous in their delight at this remarkable concert.'

Only a short while after this, Weber left Mannheim to live in Darmstadt, a town a little further up the Rhine. Here, he probably thought the opportunities would be better for him under the reigning Grand Duke Ludwig 1, who was known to be a serious musician (he was no mean performer on the piano, flute and horn). The Duke also took an active rôle in the supervision of the opera that was performed weekly. Another strong incentive was the fact that not only was his old friend Gänsbacher living there, but also the Abbé Vogler.

Weber, now 24, was markedly less impulsive than he had been in his Württemberg days. Nevertheless, he still enjoyed gaiety, and delighted in the comradeship of his closest friends. Gottfried and Dusch, who accompanied Weber to Darmstadt, joined him many times for a pleasant ramble through the wooded valleys along the Rhine or the Neckar. Weber, who had acquired considerable proficiency on the guitar, would entertain them on these jaunts with his newest songs (sung in his husky, damaged voice), which often had a strong folk-song element. In the aftermath of the Napoleonic wars and the continuing political divisions in Germany, the heady Romantics were bent on personal rediscovery. This involved not only a glance back at the heroic past, but a recognition of what was best in the unfolding present.

One of the main enthusiasms of artists and writers at the time were the songs and stories of the peasant communities. Eventually these would prove a binding factor in the unity of the nation. As John Warrack has succinctly put it: 'Folk-song and folk-tale were to prove a method of establishing national identity that was to last into our own century; in Weber's day they were an exciting novelty.'

It is perhaps relevant at this point to describe Weber's personal appearance. Max Maria recorded:

Carl Maria's person was thin, as it always was through life – small, weakly, almost insignificant – not otherwise than well-formed however, unless exception were to be taken to his long thin neck, which rose so conspicuously from his narrow shoulders. The weakness of his right hip, which later in life made him limp, was as yet not very obvious. there was much in him to charm, whether in the noble form of his somewhat lengthy head, or in his deep blue eyes – which his friends have termed 'inexhaustible fountains of kindliness and love' – or in the ever-varying expression of his face, now lightened by roguish humour or jovial enjoyment, now flushed with enthusiasm, now illuminated by profound and noble thoughts. No wonder then that many women preferred the youth to handsomer and more striking men. At this period he already wore the long black coat, the tightly-fitting pantaloons, the white neckcloth, the conspicuous shirtfrill, and the high 'cannon' boots with which his portraiture is now almost inseparable in men's minds.

Once settled in Darmstadt, Weber wasted no time in renewing his former ties with Vogler and Gänsbacher. Vogler had been persuaded to take up residence in Darmstadt by the Grand Duke Ludwig, and had been awarded a Grand Cross, the position of Privy Counsellor, plus a house with the respectable salary of over two thousand gulden. Although the old composer accepted this unexpected gesture, he found his musical advice was never asked for by the wily Duke, even in the management of the opera.

Vogler's income was further enhanced by the acquisition of a well-heeled pupil of 18 by the name of Jacob Beer, later to be known as Giacomo Meyerbeer. Although a somewhat tortuous friendship soon developed between him and Weber, in later years they drifted apart due to the differing goals and ambitions they pursued. However, Weber always remained on the best of terms with Meyerbeer's kindly parents, whose house was open to him when he went to Berlin.

For all the enjoyable times Weber, Gänsbacher and Meyerbeer had together, we find, in less than a fortnight, Weber writing to Gottfried in this vein: 'I take up my goose-quill to tell you in

The opera composer
Giacomo Meyerbeer.

boring words how bored I am with boring Darmstadt.' Little
musical life existed in the town outside that connected with the
Grand Duke.

This was not a period when Weber was inspired to compose.
True, as Max Maria tells us, the young man went 'melody
hunting', and snatched new inspiration from ditties of the day.
Out of such common tunes he would evolve his own themes,
which bore about as much resemblance to the original as the
brilliant butterfly to the dingy chrysalis. The principal ideas for
the famous *Invitation to the Dance* and for the ballet music in
Oberon were developed out of other songs in this way.

When the fun was not of a musical nature, Max Maria relates:

. . . one of their jokes they owed to Carl Maria's dog, whom he had
named 'Ma'mselle'. When a pretty girl passed in the street, 'Ma'mselle!

48

Ma'mselle!' was called, until the damsel turned, looked round, to the great delight of the young fellows, and then was made to understand that it was to the dog the name applied.

As we have seen, Weber composed a number of songs (mostly with guitar) in these mid-months of 1810. However, ideas for a new Romantic opera began running through his head following the completion, in February, of *Silvana*. Shortly before leaving Mannheim, Hiemer had given him the libretto of *Abu Hassan*, a *Singspiel* in one act based on a story from *Arabian Nights*.

With the relatively carefree days Weber was experiencing at the time, it could be imagined that this lighthearted subject would suit him well, but, for the time being, he put it aside. He did write one tune, however, which was eventually to find its way into the final score, and the way in which it got there was quite unusual.

One spring evening, when Weber was staying with his friend Dusch outside Heidelberg, he was leaning out of the window humming tunes. One of these was to become 'Ah, Fatima Beloved', but come the morning Weber had completely forgotten it. Fortunately, Dusch had taken careful note of it, and having the sly opportunity of repeating the melody, impelled Weber to fly at him, taking him by the throat, and laughingly exclaiming: 'You scoundrel! You have stolen that out of my head where I had happened to mislay it.'

It was also in Heidelberg that the two friends came across some newly-published ghost stories by Apel. The first one, entitled *Der Freischütz*, so immediately caught their imagination that Dusch set about preparing a scenario that very night. Dusch, however, had other commitments and soon found that he was too busy to write the libretto. The whole project was 'deferred' as Benedict puts it: '. . . until Weber's genius had reached its ultimate and highest development ten years later.'

During Weber's period in Darmstadt of almost exactly a year, he undertook a number of other journeys. One, through the endeavours of Vogler, included a concert at Aschaffenburg. Another was to Frankfurt in May, where the composer had the chance to explain to his old patron, Duke Eugen of Carlsruhe, the reasons for his dismissal from Stuttgart. The Duke was sympathetic and, on parting, affirmed his belief in Weber's innocence. As a gift, he gave him a valuable ring off his own finger.

Whilst in Frankfurt, Weber also took the opportunity of visiting the famous music publisher Nikolaus Simrock. Paying the composer a comparatively small sum, they agreed to publish *Der erste Ton*, the Piano Quartet, the *Grand pot-pourri* for cello and the *Grande Polonaise* in E flat. This Polonaise alone, which became very popular, made Simrock thousands of gulden.

Back in Darmstadt, Weber, along with Gänsbacher and Meyerbeer, agreed to collaborate in composing a Cantata for Vogler's sixty-first birthday. Lots were drawn, and to Weber fell the task of writing the words. Unfortunately, the homage they prepared did little to humour their old master; Vogler felt slighted by the Duke Ludwig's omission in sending any birthday message to his 'musical Privy Counsellor'.

Vogler, possibly plagued with a twinge of guilt, invited Weber to accompany him on a concert tour to Frankfurt and Mainz. Weber, with an eye to having his opera *Silvana* put into production at the Frankfurt theatre, accepted at once. These hopes came to nothing for the moment, but this setback was counterbalanced by two chance incidents that occurred in Frankfurt. One was an encounter with his old sweetheart, Margarethe Lang, who happened to be there; but times had changed – and their ardour had cooled. The other was to have the greatest significance in his life. At a concert, a young soprano named Caroline Brandt sang an aria by Paer most beautifully; Caroline was later to become Weber's wife.

Following the success of this brief tour, Weber, accompanied by Gottfried and Augusta, his wife, travelled to Baden-Baden, then already a fashionable spa. With his finances running low, Weber hoped to replenish his funds by giving a concert, but he found himself thwarted by bad luck at every turn. In an amusing letter to Gänsbacher (written some time later) Weber refers to his: '. . . evil star, who had too long allowed things to go on pleasantly not to play me some vile prank on this occasion.'

Still, the trip to Baden-Baden was not without its compensations. Besides meeting several of his Stuttgart friends, he met the poet Tieck, and most important of all, the publisher Johann Cotta, who asked him to write an article for his literary and social journal *Morgenblatt*. It is significant that Cotta, who had been responsible for publishing most of the great German classics, should have made this request. In the previous year, 1809, Weber had started on his semi-autobiographical novel *'Tonkünstlers Leben'* and had had one episode published entitled *Fragment of a Musical Journey*. Although he was to work sporadically on the novel until 1820, he never completed it. Some of the novel deals with aesthetics, albeit in an amusing and entertaining fashion. Here Weber lampoons both critics and the public in a brilliant manner. He does this by forming a dialogue between two fictitious characters called Diehl and Felix. It's a method not unlike that which Oscar Wilde was to adopt much later in the century with his *The Critic as Artist* – a dialogue where the two characters are Gilbert and Ernest.

In his introduction to *Carl Maria von Weber: Writings on Music*,

Johann Cotta, the publisher of
the literary and social journal
Morgenblatt.

Ludwig Tieck, poet, editor
and translator.

Warrack refers to Weber's style in his early essays as having 'an
infectious enthusiasm'. Warrack then goes on to quote one of
Weber's own notes attached to *Tonkünstlers Leben*, where he
admits that his enthusiasm can become somewhat exaggerated. It
gives a valuable and interesting insight into the workings of a
creative musician.

I find my style highly coloured and – because its intention is to give an
exhaustive account – slightly precious and bombastic. However, I cannot
divorce myself from it, however much I may respect and be deeply
devoted to the clarity of a Goethe, a Schlegel or a Tieck. Perhaps it may
be my very musicality that accounts for it. The many descriptive
adjectives in a language closely resemble the instrumentation of a musical
idea. I am conscious of being able to reproduce such an idea with just as
much clarity as I conceived it, though this is very seldom true of ideas
which I wish to express in words.

In sheer volume Weber's writings about his life and music in general are unparalleled by any significant composer in Western music not excepting Berlioz. More importantly, his writings give proof of how many-sided and highly articulate a person Weber was. It is a tragedy, therefore, that following the bicentenary of his birth in 1986, Weber's diary, which he kept assiduously from February 1810 until two days before his death in June 1826, has still not been published in its entirety. The diary fills seven volumes, and gives a detailed record of his day-to-day life, actions and thoughts, notes on the progress of his works, and even particulars of his expenditure. Contrary to Weber's wishes it was kept intact by his wife after his death. Eventually it passed into the hands of Weber's great-great-grandson who let it be known in 1986 that it was unlikely to be published for another ten years.

Chapter 9

Weber's 'Evil Star' in the Ascendant Again

With the idea of furthering the cause of Romantic music, Weber founded the *Harmonische Verein* (The Harmonic Society) in the autumn of 1810. This was a secret club given over to:

. . . bring forward genuine talent wherever it might be found, and at the same time to warn the world of all that was false or bad in art, however much supported it might be for unworthy motives by the critical authorities of the day.

Weber, with his flair for organisation, was the leader; he formulated the 21 statutes that were drawn up. Gottfried became the treasurer, secretary and archivist. Pseudonyms were given to each member and appeared as signatures to their literary work. Weber was 'Melos' (or 'M-s'), and Gottfried was 'G. Giusto'. Other members included Meyerbeer, Dusch, Gänsbacher, Danzi, and the clarinettist, Berner. One thing they eschewed was any thought of being considered a mutual admiration society. Of the many reviews that survive by the members of the society only six refer to one of their own works.

Unfortunately, although the ideas of the society reflected a real need (musical criticism in Germany at the time was not of the highest order), the busy lives of the main protagonists gave them little opportunity to build it up, and interest slowly waned. By 1813 the society was virtually defunct.

Towards the end of August 1810, Weber travelled to Frankfurt to conduct the long-awaited production of his opera *Silvana*. Margarethe Lang was, at that time, a member of the Frankfurt opera; she had already appeared in Cherubini's *Lodoiska*, where she had impressed the audience with her grace, fine acting and dramatic sense. Weber had written the part of Mechtilde in *Silvana* specially for her.

The name part of Silvana, the dumb girl, was to be taken by the charming Caroline Brandt, whom he had already admired at a concert in Frankfurt. Max Maria describes her in detail:

. . . her grace of movement, joined to her sylph-like figure and her little feet, made men regret she was not a dancer; whilst her pretty drollery, her simple-minded dash of manner, and her sweet natural coquetry, excited the desire to see her talent confined to the dramatic stage alone. But then her highly sympathetic, admirably-trained soprano voice was so remarkable that it would have been a sin if she had not been an opera singer.

At this point, it would appear that neither Caroline Brandt nor Weber had any special feelings for one another, though he immediately recognised her talent, whilst she admired the young composer.

The *Silvana* rehearsals went smoothly, and everything seemed to augur well, when an unforeseen problem arose. On the very day of the opera's première, 16 September 1810, Madame Blanchard, widow of the pioneering balloonist Jean-Pierre Blanchard, was to make a balloon ascent. Balloon ascents in those days were sensational events which concentrated the interest of the public to the exclusion of anything else. Consequently, although Weber's friends from all around came to support him, the theatre was nowhere near full. Worse, the audience was plainly preoccupied with the ascent, and their excited chatter soon seriously distracted the singers. Nevertheless, although the opera didn't go as well as it had in the dress rehearsal, there were several encores. Eventually Caroline Brandt managed to persuade the unwilling composer onto the stage to acknowledge the applause.

Today, *Silvana* is worthy of our attention, at least in concert performance, for the brilliance of the scoring, some of the vocal numbers, and the fact that a proportion of it (how much is not known) stems from his earlier opera *Das Waldmädchen*, of which only fragments survive. *Silvana* was the first of Weber's operas to achieve success, and the earliest to be translated, in this case, into English.

If Weber was disappointed with the outcome of *Silvana*, he didn't flinch from extracting part of one of the arias and making it the subject of variations for the first movement of his Fifth Violin Sonata, op.10. This was one of Six Progressive Sonatas Weber wrote, involving much toil and sweat, to fulfil a commission by the publishers André. Although hardly displaying the wealth of melodic invention that characterises Schubert's Three Sonatinas (composed six years later), they do have a vitality and charm of their own. Some time after depositing the completed sonatas with

Madame Blanchard making a balloon ascent in Paris in June 1810.

André, he was told they had been rejected because, so he wrote to Gottfried, 'they were too good, and must be made more ordinary for sale'.

In October 1810, Weber completed his Piano Concerto no. 1, the most ambitious work he had so far written for his instrument. It has infectiously joyful themes in the outer movements – the Presto-finale, for instance, contains chirpy waltz sections within its rondo structure. It's a brilliant piece of piano writing. The first movement, with its military overtones (and Napoleonic reminders), has some striking harmonic changes. But the most interesting movement of this admittedly uneven work is the Adagio. Over the dark colours of the lower strings, Weber weaves the piano part in a delicate tracery which, with its use of

55

decoration, clearly foreshadows Chopin. However, Weber was not alone, at this time, in adopting the highly embellished style of writing that Chopin was to develop so strikingly at a later date. Apart from John Field (his first Nocturne was to be published in 1812), Ferdinand Ries, the brilliant pianist pupil of Beethoven, was to write a Clarinet Trio (1811), a Septet and Clarinet Duo (both 1812), that in their slow movements all anticipated in the piano writing this preference for extended decorative figuration.

Weber found life in Darmstadt tedious and dreary without his jovial friend Gänsbacher, who had taken up a new post in Prague. What's more, the 'indefatigable young Meyerbeer was far too diligently employed to afford him much companionship.' Weber took refuge in hard work, concentrating on completing *Abu Hassan*.

Then an invitation from Gottfried arrived, asking him to come and help organise a concert in Mannheim in honour of the Grand Duchess Stephanie of Baden. Weber jumped at the chance of getting away from Darmstadt, and early in November was reunited with his old friend. For the concert, which was a great success, Weber played his Piano Concerto in its entirety for the first time.

Then efforts were made by certain factions to have the opera conductor, Peter Ritter, who had been neglecting his duties more and more, pensioned off and replaced by Weber. This backfired when Ritter learned of the attempt to dislodge him. With relations soured not only between Weber and Ritter, but with the whole orchestra, who probably feared that a new conductor would mean an increase in their workload, Weber's position in Mannheim became untenable.

Max Maria tells us that on his last evening he sat at the piano, in Dusch's room, with sunken head and full eyes, and extemporised that exquisitely pathetic song 'Des Künstlers Abschied' (The Artist's Farewell).

With his 'evil star' seemingly in the ascendant, Weber retraced his steps to Darmstadt. Suddenly, a chink of light beckoned the dejected composer. Finishing *Abu Hassan* on 11 January 1811, Vogler suggested that Weber should dedicate it to the Grand Duke Ludwig, which Weber duly did. 'I have dressed up the fellow in smart red binding,' he writes to Gottfried, 'and sent him, with the due dedication, to the Grand Duke. Who knows what he will say? Perhaps, if he is in good humour, "Mussje, je tiens bocup de ce".' (Weber adds, mimicking the Duke's poor French).

It is possible that Vogler, aware of Weber's misfortunes, had spoken with his patron, the Grand Duke, for the dedication was accepted. Moreover, a purse containing 40 gold pieces was sent to Weber along with the offer of a concert. The Grand Duke and

Duchess both promised to grace the occasion, and duly bought no fewer than 120 tickets for the court.

But it had been a hard and bitter year for Weber. Though the concert was a success in every way, there was no future for him in Darmstadt. Talk of his becoming a Grand Ducal Musical Director soon faded. As Max Maria puts it: '. . . on second thoughts, the Grand Duke, like Ritter and Mannheim, seemed to fear the energy and talent of a spirited young man.'

On 12 February, Gottfried, Dusch and Meyerbeer bade their last farewells to Weber, who wrote in his diary under that date: 'Shall I ever again find in the world friends so dear, and men so true?' 16 years later, shortly before his death, he wrote opposite this entry: 'NO!'

Obviously a change of scene was needed to counter his morbid introspection, and, two days later, Weber left Darmstadt 'fortified with a mass of letters of introduction which the royal couple had lavishly showered on him.' The idea was to make an extended concert tour – a 'great artistic journey' – which would show the world what a virtuoso he was. The list of cities to be visited was impressive – Munich, Prague, Dresden, Berlin, Copenhagen, and St Petersburg. In the event, the area covered was much smaller, coming to a stop at the first mentioned, Munich. But first Weber came upon the university town of Giessen where he found the

A tavern c. 1810.

57

A self-portrait by
E.T.A. Hoffmann.
Underneath is written
'überaus ähnlich'.
('Absolutely true to life').

student population 'already knew and loved his catchy German melodies'. After playing in a few private circles, his reputation as a pianist spread like wildfire through the little town. So great was the curiosity and so overpowering the crowd which flocked round him, that he began to grow weary of what he called his 'undeserved honours'. The very porters, who carried his pianoforte to the concert-room and back, refused all remuneration after the performance.

Then he travelled on, through Aschaffenburg and Würzburg, arriving in Bamberg on 3 March. Here, a chance meeting with a person attached to the theatre was to have a significant influence on Weber's later life. One evening, while sipping 'cool Franconian wine' in *Die Rose*, Weber fell into conversation with two men seated at a nearby table. One of them turned out to be the Musical Director E.T.A. Hoffmann, who was to become one of Germany's most celebrated writers, with his weird and uncanny stories. Weber was almost mesmerised by the Romantic aura of this wild-looking individual with his 'diabolical flashes of lightning wit'. An uneasy relationship, however, was to mark their future meetings.

Eventually, Weber reached Munich on 14 March and he rented a modest apartment. He was to remain in the city for some five months.

Chapter 10

1811 and a Great Clarinettist

Munich, now capital of the new Kingdom of Bavaria, was seeing the beginnings of a resurgence of interest in the arts under Maximilian I and his minister Maximilian Josef von Montgelas. Weber had with him a letter of introduction to this minister, and, as a result, was granted an interview with the Queen, who, expressing a desire to hear him play, promised a concert. Another such letter was addressed to Karl Friedrich von Wiebeking, the director of public works, whose original ideas on architecture delighted Weber. At Wiebeking's home, Weber came to feel like one of the family, and, to return the kindness and hospitality he received there, gave piano lessons to the daughter of the house. Here too, Weber met the clarinettist Heinrich Bärmann again.

Bärmann was two years older than Weber and, as a child, had been sent to the School for Military Music in Potsdam. At the age of 11 he began to play the clarinet. Later, Bärmann had the good fortune to receive tuition from both Joseph Beer and Franz Tausch, the first two great virtuosi on the instrument. In October 1806, with the advance of Napoleon, Bärmann, as soldier as well as bandsman, was obliged to spearhead his regiment at the battle of Jena, blowing his clarinet the whole time to sustain the morale of the troops. He was captured and experienced privations of the most appalling kind throughout a hard winter, until he was lucky enough to escape. Relieved of the necessity to fight for his country, Bärmann eventually succeeded in reaching Munich. Here, he was invited to play before King Maximilian, whereupon his success was so great that he was immediately engaged as first clarinet in the court orchestra, a position he held until his death in 1847. A concert tour through Switzerland and Southern France in 1808 brought him wide recognition and fame.

Weber asked Bärmann to perform something at the concert he was putting on for the Queen, and Bärmann agreed, providing Weber produced a new solo piece for him to play. Weber went into action at once, and, within three days, composed his Concertino

Maximilian I.

for clarinet and orchestra. The concert, set for 5 April, was a
sell-out, with the whole court attending. Undoubtedly, the
première of the Concertino was the high spot for the audience,
who were enthralled by the clarinettist's wonderful playing and
'marvellous charm'. But it was a personal triumph for Weber
too, for the 87-strong orchestra was rapturous in its applause for
the composer.

This concert cemented a friendship which was to last for the rest
of their lives. Max Maria relates:

In their communion as artists, or in long years of separation, never was this friendship weakened. With much similarity of character, no two men could have been more dissimilar in personal appearance; Weber thin, pale, weakly; Bärmann tall, athletic, with a magnificently handsome head. Carl Maria would laughingly say of the personal advantages of his friend – 'All the choicest tit-bits in life are presented to that handsome fellow on a silver platter; poor devils like me must beg for the crumbs which fall from his Magnificence's table.'

After the success of the Concertino, the King commissioned Weber to compose two full-scale clarinet concertos.

The clarinet was Weber's favourite wind instrument. Ever since *Peter Schmoll*, it had figured conspicuously in many of his compositions. The distinctive mellow tone of the lower register particularly appealed to him, with its romantic and dramatic possibilities and this was to be fully exploited in his imminent solo clarinet works, and still later in the overtures to *Der Freischütz* and *Oberon*.

Bärmann had recently acquired a ten-keyed boxwood instrument. This not only gave him greater agility and smoothness, but helped him to produce that richness of tone that, allied to his superior artistry, made him unequalled in his day.

The court orchestra at Munich was a good one – some of its members were famous players from the celebrated Mannheim orchestra of Mozart's time, who had followed the court to Munich in 1778. Their conductor was Peter Winter, a man with whom Weber was never to be on friendly terms. Carl Maria writes to Gottfried:

The members of the orchestra are mighty grand fellows, and as arrogant as you please; but they have taken it into their heads to pet me amazingly. That envious old Winter has been uncommonly diverting. When I first paid him a visit, he took me for a dilettante, and overpowered me with politeness; but when, after a day or two, he discovered how matters stood, he was so abominably rude that all the musicians called him a beast. How a man, who has already earned his laurels can so tarnish them by letting himself down in this manner, I don't know.

Following the success of his concert, Weber was asked to write concertos for numerous other instruments of the orchestra, but only one was to materialise. Not surprisingly, considering his mind was preoccupied with wind instruments, this was a Bassoon Concerto for Georg Friedrich Brandt, a Munich player. He did find time, however, to publish an article called 'A New Discovery for Perfecting the Flute', which gives an enthusiastic account of Nepomuk Capeller's ingenious invention to increase the range of the instrument 'without prejudice to the equal purity of all the

61

notes and intervals.' Weber's musical interests were certainly wide-ranging.

As Max Maria records of this time – 'On every side he was in demand.' In a letter to Gottfried, the composer admits that his 'earnings are pretty considerable.' Even the envious and rude Winter suddenly became all 'friendliness and politeness', indicating that a higher influence had been brought to bear on him. Then, from Winter himself, Weber was told that *Abu Hassan* 'was to be put into immediate rehearsal'. It would seem that the important turning-point in Weber's career was at hand. Unbelievably, even Württemberg, which had banished Weber into exile, was planning a production of the opera (suppressing his name however).

In Munich, whilst rehearsals went well, Weber found time to dally with the female members of the company who employed every trick of coquetry to win the heart of the rising star. At this time, there is often to be found in Weber's diary the abbreviation 'A.W.T.N.' – *Alle Weiber taugen nichts* – (all women are worthless), though it must be said that it is difficult to believe that he actively discouraged their advances!

The first performance of *Abu Hassan* took place on 4 June 1811 in Munich's *Hofbühne* before a capacity audience. It was a great success. Following the overture, a dramatic moment occurred when a cry of 'fire' went up, creating pandemonium in the hall. When it was found to be a false alarm, the performance continued, and no less than five numbers were encored.

Taking Mozart's *Entführung* as its model, *Abu Hassan* brims with vitality. Full of sparkling music with racy tunes, the story is often hilariously funny. It is ironic to reflect that the main subject matter of the story is to do with debt and moneylenders, a scenario with which Weber was intimately acquainted! Of the stage works before *Der Freischütz*, it is the only Weber opera that enjoys the occasional revival today.

On 9 June, Weber's friend Max Heigel, the actor and poet, died. For his funeral, Weber wrote the *Trauer-Musik*. However, Winter's Requiem was played instead, much to Weber's bitter disappointment. It must be said, though, that Weber's piece only lasts about seven minutes, and its brevity may well have been the reason for the substitution of Winter's work, rather than the scheming of Heigel's son as asserted by Weber. The *Trauer-Musik*, which, as far as is known, received its first performance in Oxford as recently as 1986, is divided into three main sections. Apart from the close, which is a re-scoring of the earlier choral 'Grablied' (1803), the music is new and shows great intensity of expression. The composer's handling of the forces involved (baritone solo, chorus, ten wind instruments and timpani) is always resourceful. The middle section, a recitative and aria for baritone solo, has one of Weber's most gently lilting melodies to words that start – 'Death has snatched from our midst the friend whose art and life both delighted us . . .'

On 13 June, two new works by Weber were performed at a concert sponsored by Friedrich Kaufmann, the Dresden piano maker: the Clarinet Concerto no. 1 with Bärmann as soloist, and an Adagio and Rondo for harmonichord and orchestra. Constructed in 1809 by Kaufmann (who had since learnt to play it expertly), the harmonichord attempted to overcome the normal dissipation of sound on the piano of the time, by means of a rosined wheel coming into contact with the strings. However, Weber's enthusiasm for the instrument quickly waned with the many problems he had when he came to write for it.

After being offered the post of *Kapellmeister* at Wiesbaden, and eventually turning it down because the money wasn't good enough, Weber set off on 9 August for a trip to Switzerland.

Deciding to risk travelling through part of the kingdom of Württemberg from which he had been exiled, Weber was unlucky enough to be recognised by a former Stuttgart Chief Inspector. After being confined to a room in an inn for three days, the decision was finally taken to have him escorted to Mörsburg and put on a boat for Constance. As this was precisely the direction in which he wanted to go, Weber can't have worried very much.

Eventually he arrived at Schaffhausen, where he met up with the Meyerbeer family, and, after hearing two concerts promoted by the Swiss Music Society, moved on with them to Winterthur. Having been advised to give a concert in the town, Weber chose to perform his Piano Concerto no. 1, but the orchestra, consisting of amateurs, was so poor that he felt obliged to rearrange it for piano and string quartet! Moving on to Zürich after this unprofitable and frustrating experience, and there finding Nägeli still unwilling to publish the planned journal of the *Harmonische Verein*, Weber, in a letter to Gottfried confessed:

On 2 September I had a marvellous idea which I've immediately put into effect. I intend, by means of a little guidebook, to help travelling artists to overcome the usual endless trouble with arrangements for a concert when one doesn't know whom to turn to, who can help, what music's popular etc.

He followed up this idea in a letter to Gänsbacher a little later:

The book will cover Germany in the widest sense, and I'll contribute a survey of the artistic situation in every district and every town. I enclose a plan set out as a questionnaire and request you to answer it thoroughly about Prague . . .

With this idea, Weber was foreshadowing the rôle of the modern-day concert promoter. Envisaging the book to cover a large part of Europe, Weber prepared an interesting report on Basel when he returned to Lake Constance in October. It is, perhaps, noteworthy that of the smaller countries Denmark was proposed but England was not included. Unfortunately, the book was never completed.

Weber's preoccupation with this *Handbook for Wandering Musical Artists* might have meant the neglect of his other musical activities, but we find that on 24 September he had started work on a Clarinet Quintet for Bärmann, whilst a guest of his friend the Bavarian Minister Count Olry.

Weber returned home to Munich by way of Lindau, cautiously skirting the troublesome kingdom of Württemberg. He had been away three months. During this time his reputation and self-confidence had grown steadily, and his health had improved in the bracing Swiss mountain air. Mentally too, he had gained. In his diary he notes: 'A man should not attempt to describe these wonders.' And in a letter to Dusch he writes: 'Am I to describe the scenery? Such an attempt would drive me completely mad. No! I can feel in God's free nature; but speak of it I cannot.' In Switzerland, all Weber's Rousseau-like Romantic notions came to the fore.

Back in Munich, Weber was overjoyed to learn from Bärmann that a joint tour was actively being arranged for the north of Germany. It was an idea that Weber readily fell in with, all the more because his 'multifarious love-adventures' were causing him complications. But first there were many things to be seen to: critical literary notices to write; and a group of three canzonets to be completed for presentation to the Queen. Most importantly, he had to prepare a grand concert, to be given before his final departure.

Weber, now frantically busy, completed, on 8 November, the overture *Der Beherrscher der Geister*, which was a reworking of the now lost *Rübezahl* overture. The concert, due for 25 November, would be attended by the royal couple, and was also to include an improvisation by Weber on the piano, and the concert aria 'Miser a me'. This had been composed for the beautiful Madame Peyermann, whilst Weber was staying with Count Olry. The concert was not only a great success, but a touching affair. As Max Maria writes: 'It was impossible for the artist to bid farewell more overwhelmed with honour and glory, than did Weber in his adieu to Munich.'

But there was one further concert, and it involved Bärmann, who premièred the composer's Clarinet Concerto no. 2 – playing, according to Weber's diary, 'in a heavenly manner'.

Chapter 11

1812: a Year of Wandering

On 1 December, Weber and Bärmann set off on their tour with joyful spirits. Between them, they had procured a comfortable carriage and, travelling day and night, they arrived in Prague four days later. Weber, though utterly exhausted, was happy to be greeted by his dear friend Gänsbacher, who was residing in the city in the service of Count Firmian.

At this time, Prague, like the whole of Bohemia, was under the yoke of the Austrian Hapsburgs who, well into the nineteenth century, relied on the repressive methods of a police state. All attempts at revivifying Czech music and literature were frowned upon, or even thought to be seditious. Fortunately, the nobility still treasured Bohemia's musical tradition and actively encouraged music-making. In 1810, eight nobles had founded a *Verein zur Beförderung der Tonkunst in Böhmen* (Society for the Advancement of Music in Bohemia) and this society opened its own music school during the year of Weber's arrival. It was therefore not surprising that Gänsbacher, with the backing of Count Firmian, was successful in obtaining sponsorship from many of the nobility in Prague.

Gänsbacher had arranged a concert, which was to take place in Count Firmian's house on 14 December. The night before their appearance some local dilettanti extracted a promise from Weber and Bärmann, that they would perform a duet together, though they had only solo pieces with them. Early the following morning, Weber hit on the idea of using the theme from his opera *Silvana* again (the same one he had already reworked in his Fifth Violin Sonata). Working with speed, a set of Variations (J.128) were finished by midday, Bärmann himself contributing an Adagio variation (Bärmann, in the years ahead, was to become the composer of a number of clarinet works). At the concert in the evening, the piece was greeted with repeated cries of 'Bravo!'.

Weber, in the meantime, had visited Liebich, the Director of the theatre in Prague. Most of the administration of Liebich's admirably-organised theatre was conducted at his bedside, as he suffered from a kidney complaint. Max Maria relates:

When Carl Maria entered the sick-room, Liebich stretched out his hand to him with a benevolent smile and said, 'So you are THE Weber! A capital fellow, I hear, and a very devil on the piano. So you want me to buy your operas? Very well – I understand they're good. One fills an evening, the other doesn't, I'll give you 1500 gulden for the two. How's that?'

Weber readily accepted, and promised that he would return to Prague for rehearsals the following spring.

After another successful concert on 21 December, which included the First Clarinet Concerto and the Piano Concerto, Weber and Bärmann left for Dresden. Here, there was little they could do as the court was absent and, continuing their journey, they arrived in Leipzig on the 27th. Rochlitz, the celebrated critic,

The music critic
Johann Friedrich Rochlitz.

who had encouraged Weber from the beginning, lived here and, as Weber had never met him, it was natural he should seek him out. Rochlitz received him with the greatest friendliness and took the trouble to introduce him to important personages, but without much result. The Seconda brothers, who managed the Leipzig and Dresden theatres, were mainly interested in Italian opera, so he could expect little support from them. However, a visit to the music publishers Härtel and Kühnel was more productive.

With Leipzig itself, Weber was disappointed, thinking it a dull and uninteresting town in comparison with Prague – 'Beer, tobacco and bowls are all they live for here', he wrote in disgust. Turning to literary work for consolation, he started another chapter of his novel *Tonkünstlers Leben*. He was hard at work on this when, unexpectedly, a letter arrived from the Duke of Gotha, inviting him to visit his court for a while. The idea excited Weber's interest, for he had heard that Napoleon had declared the Duke to be one of the most talented princes in Germany. With Bärmann, Weber set off for Gotha on 17 January 1812.

The Duke, Emil Leopold of Saxe-Gotha, though brought up in the strictest military discipline, was a warm and genuinely enthusiastic devotee of all branches of art. He was also an eccentric, sometimes appearing before his bewildered court in a lady's gown as his official dress, and frequently with different coloured hair. But he had a whimsical and inventive sense of humour: once, on hearing a tune too cheerful in the major key and too solemn in the minor, he requested it to be half-major!

On their arrival, the two musicians were taken aback to find his Lordship absent, though Spohr, the resident *Konzertmeister* in Gotha, was there, embarking on his first oratorio. The Duke re-appeared a few days later, and commandeered their attentions relentlessly. Max Maria relates:

Melodies had to be improvised on the piano or guitar to the Duke's poetry. Impromptu performances had to be hastily arranged for Spohr and Bärmann.

Eventually, Weber, exhausted by the demands made on him, and perhaps put out by Spohr's thinly veiled contempt for him as an artist, hurriedly left Gotha with Bärmann on 27 January.

Their next stop was Weimar. With letters of introduction to the Grand Duchess Maria Paulowna, sister of the Russian Tsar, preparations were soon in hand for a series of musical evenings in her palace.

It was on one of these evenings, when Weber and Bärmann were performing the *Silvana* Variations, that Goethe entered, sat down, and began talking loudly to a lady until the music stopped,

Duke Emil Leopold of Saxe-Gotha.

at which point he left. Later, Weber was presented to Goethe but the great man affected little interest. It is possible that Goethe, who had some influence in operatic circles in Weimar and was known to favour the rigidly disciplined school of theatrical declamation, sensed the contrary flow of Romantic indulgence in Weber. Certainly, any operatic ambitions Weber might have had whilst in Weimar were forlorn – the Grand Duchess attempted to have *Silvana* staged, but it came to nothing. On the other hand, Weber's meeting with Alexander Wolff, who had written a number of Spanish plays, was to bear fruit later. Weber was to provide incidental music for his play *Preciosa* in 1822.

It was not long before the two musicians left for Berlin. Here, Weber was made most welcome in the home of Meyerbeer's parents.

The gloomy political atmosphere of Berlin prior to the universal uprising of the nation against the French invader, awoke in Weber a political awareness that identified itself with the love of country embodied in the word 'Fatherland'. For Weber, who had spent his life wandering through numerous little German states, the feeling and, indeed, meaning of the word 'Fatherland' had never

Berlin.

been in any way developed. With Weber's introduction to *Liedertafel*, a society promoting vocal music which was founded by Carl Zelter in 1808, a new focus was found for his growing nationalistic tendency. These clubs, which soon multiplied during the political depression of Napoleon's rule in Germany, were built round the social conviviality of drinking, eating and even talking (so long as silence was respected during the singing) – something which would have been to Weber's liking. For the *Liedertafel*, Weber composed an energetic cantata entitled *Das Turnierbankett* for two male-voice choirs, which exactly reflected the mood of patriotism surfacing in Berlin. It achieved huge success through its freshness and originality and, according to Max Maria, was even praised by the cantankerous Zelter, who had not been very forthcoming when he first met the composer. *Das Turnierbankett* was the first of many patriotic songs in which Weber was to succeed in catching the spirit of the slowly coalescing German nation, determined to throw off its foreign shackles. Max Maria was certainly on the right lines when he wrote that Weber 'possessed the peculiar art of hearing his own works with the ears of the masses'. Perhaps this is why Weber has retained a special place in the hearts of the German people and why, through the years, so many books about him have appeared in the German language.

But Weber's lengthy stay in Berlin was not all success. Much intrigue and opposition had to be overcome before his opera *Silvana* was eventually put into rehearsal, and, even then, there were doubts as to whether it would actually be performed and whether Weber would be allowed to conduct it. Finally, with the composer conducting, it was produced on 10 July, and was an enormous success. After all the in-fighting, Weber was relieved and grateful, writing in his diary:

Thank heaven, despite all the cabals, the good cause has won the day! Even my enemies now confess that I have genius; and now, although I feel and acknowledge my defects, I will not lose self control, but march on with courage on the path of art, although with circumspection and watchfulness over self.

With the Berlin production of *Silvana*, Weber had certainly needed to develop his sense of self-criticism. Even his Berlin friend, Friedrich von Drieberg, had levelled, though kindly enough, an accusation of 'wearisome monotony' about the work during the early rehearsal stage. Weber's revisions to the opera, including substituting two new arias (with new texts) served to improve it: the 'pacing' was tightened and the melodies themselves became more vocal in character. But a note in Weber's diary discloses:

69

I must watch over my style so as not to become monotonous . . . in my melodies the sustaining of notes is too frequent and too conspicuous . . . with regard to tempo and rhythm, I must seek in the future more variety.

Work on the revision of *Silvana* afforded Weber some distraction from the terrible news that his father had passed away in Mannheim on 16 April, aged 78. For all the problems old Anton had brought his son, Weber had loved his father deeply, recognising that, for all his meddling and pompous conceit, his father had genuinely loved him. Suddenly aware of his loss, Weber wrote in his diary:

. . . it is an almost intolerable pain to me to think that I have not been able to bestow on him happier days. God bless him for the great love he bore me, which I so little deserved, and for the education he gave me.

In a letter to Rochlitz, Weber, bemoaning his loss and admitting his itinerant life wrote:

I am now indeed alone; the consolation that I may still have a home in a friend's heart is my only support. You are right, I know; this perpetual wandering cannot be good for me. But how can I do otherwise than seek a fitting arena for the true exercise of my art? For the moment I must go on my weary way, doing my best.

Feverish activity on musical and literary pursuits prevented him from falling into despair. Apart from *Das Turnierbankett*, he wrote a number of solo songs including the passionate *Sonett* 'Du Lieber holdes himmelsüsses Wesen' (J.130) and 'Lenz erwacht' (J.131) for six voices and piano, and another chorus for the birthday of old Beer (Meyerbeer), the banker.

But Weber did make new friends in Berlin. The most important of them was a Professor of Zoology who had just returned from exploring Southern Africa, Heinrich Lichtenstein. Co-director of the Berlin *Singakademie*, the amiable Lichtenstein was distinguished as much for his musical knowledge as his scientific attainments. Having first met at the *Singakademie*, Lichtenstein writes in his memoir:

When all was over, we walked away together. So charming was Weber's conversation, so prepossessing the manner in which he discoursed on art in general . . . that it was impossible to say 'Goodbye', and we remained together until late into the night.

This friendship was to continue for the rest of their lives.

Towards the end of August, Weber departed from Berlin,

The zoologist Heinrich Lichtenstein.

enriched by his experiences there, even if everything had not turned out to plan. He appreciated the serious professional approach to music in the city, which was in marked contrast to the dilettantism of towns like Munich and Mannheim. What he didn't know, was that he had begun to pave the way for his eventual triumph in Berlin nine years later with *Der Freischütz*.

Chapter 12

Gotha

By way of Leipzig, where Weber at last managed to sell some of his music to the publisher Kühnel (including *Der Beherrscher der Geister* overture and the Clarinet Concerto no. 2), he once again, on 6 September 1812, set foot in Gotha at the invitation of the eccentric Duke of Saxe-Gotha.

Weber was lodged in the palace of Prince Friedrich, the Duke's brother. 'Let the blue chamber in the corner next to the street be prepared for him', the Prince stipulated, 'and a piano, which must be hired, placed in the room; pen, ink and paper, and lights of course'.

But Weber was allowed little time for composition. If it wasn't the Duke hustling him from one place of residence to another at a moment's notice, or if he wasn't having to accompany the Duke's poems with improvised melodramatic music on the piano or guitar, then it was the Prince, a great lover of Italian opera, demanding that Weber sit at the piano, for half a day at a time, and accompany singers through the scores. (It is interesting to note that in May of this year Rossini's *La Scala di Seta* was first produced, unsuccessfully, in Venice, while in September *La Pietra del Paragone* was given at La Scala, Milan where it enjoyed enormous success. The Finale includes the first occasion on which Rossini employed his famous *crescendo*.)

Small wonder, then, that Weber should have yearned for the more sober intellectual life of Berlin, and the friends he had left behind. In a letter to Lichtenstein he confesses: '. . . by the constant indulgence of a pleasant dream, I feel not parted from you, but that I am only on a ramble, and must soon return home.'

But there were times when the Duke was away for a period and Weber was left to concentrate on composition. He was thus able to complete his Piano Concerto no. 2 in E flat (J.155), one of his most impressive instrumental works. He had, in fact, written the Rondo whilst in Munich the previous autumn, performing it on one occasion as the Finale to his Piano Concerto no. 1 although, as

Lithograph of Weber by Feckert.

he admitted in a letter to Gottfried at the time, 'it has a completely different character . . .'

At the beginning of December, having remained in Gotha for some three months, Weber realised it was time he continued his travels. This time, he was impelled not just by *Wanderlust*, but by necessity. Franz Anton had left debts behind him which Weber, with the honour of his beloved father at stake, recognised as his own. He had little money and was never going to make himself financially independent by staying on in Gotha, no matter how much the Duke and his family lavished their kindness on him.

So, on 17 December, Weber played his new piano concerto,

along with a number of smaller pieces. (He recorded in his diary that it 'met with wild acclaim and went excellently'.) Then, on 19 December, he set out for Leipzig, and arrived there on the 26th. Immediately, he began preparations for the New Year's Day première of the Hymn *In seiner Ordnung* for soloists, chorus and orchestra, which he had composed in Gotha to words by Rochlitz, his Leipzig admirer. At the concert, his new piano work was again a success, while his diary reports that the Hymn 'went well until the Choral, where Mlle. Campagnuoli sang so horribly flat that I came out in a cold sweat; nevertheless it was much applauded'. Having successfully sold some more of his works, including the *Rübezahl* overture and the Clarinet Concertino, to Kühnel, Weber, early in January 1813 set his sights on Prague. This he intended to be the first stop on a two-year tour of Italy, Switzerland and France.

Chapter 13

Prague

When Weber arrived in Prague on 12 January 1813, he little realised that his wandering days were virtually over. Wenzel Müller, the prolific Moravian composer, had just resigned the directorship of the Opera, and Gänsbacher soon acquainted Weber with the news that Liebich wanted him to assume the post. At first, Weber was not inclined to accept but, with Gänsbacher's persuasive arguments and Liebich's insistence, he finally gave in; at least here was a chance to discharge his father's debts.

The generous terms offered were a salary of two thousand gulden (to commence immediately), a benefit guaranteed at one thousand gulden, three months' annual leave, and absolute

Prague c. 1820.

authority to reorganise the company. The contract was to stand for three years.

There was much to be done. Under Wenzel Müller's directorship, standards had fallen and this was not entirely due to problems arising from the unsettled political situation; artistic considerations had been neglected – the taste of the public was not being satisfied, and audiences were dwindling.

In a letter to Rochlitz written soon after accepting the appointment, Weber forthrightly declared:

Never! – and I lay my hand solemnly on my heart as I say it – never shall the confidence placed in me be misused for unworthy purposes. Should I ever appear to you to be swerving from the true path of art, hold up these lines before me to my shame. They are a sacred contract between me and art, which I shall strive to fulfil with all my power to my last breath.

At first, Weber's time was spent renewing his contacts with the influential musical fraternity of Prague, amongst whom were Prince Lobkowitz, the banker Kleinwächter and Count Pachta, who had backed the recent foundation of the Conservatory – it was vital to have them on his side. The theatre in Prague had a brief but distinguished history (the zenith being the commissioning of Mozart's *Don Giovanni*), and Weber's appointment to such an eminent position naturally created a certain amount of jealousy in some quarters. After a successful concert of his music on 6 March (which included his First Symphony and Piano Concerto no. 2) he confessed to Rochlitz:

I have adversaries in plenty, but I don't let these gentlemen bother me. If I get any truth from them, I make a mental note and disregard the rest. Tomašek and Co. have been pulling wry faces ever since they knew I was to remain here . . . My whole life through I have owed much to hostility, inasmuch as it has always been my best spur to excellence.

Weber's 'spur' now, with the disbandment of the old company at Easter, was to find new talent in the way of singers and instrumentalists, to open the new season in September. With this object in view, he was about to leave for Vienna when, by a strange coincidence, he received a letter from Caroline Brandt, informing him that she was just then without an engagement. Remembering with pleasure her admirable performance in the name part of *Silvana*, he engaged her as the very first member of his new company, little dreaming that within a few years she would become his wife.

Arriving in Vienna at the end of March, Weber was overjoyed to find many of his musical friends there. 'Brother Bärmann', Spohr and 'Little Bear' Meyerbeer – now 17 years old and studying with Hummel – were all there. Unfortunately, Meyerbeer was distancing himself from his old friends. In a letter to Gottfried, Weber admits:

There is no getting on with Beer. I met him with the old heartiness and affection . . . but my old trust in him is gone. Bärmann, and especially Vogler, complain that his pride and susceptibility are such as to repel everyone from him.

At this time Weber also met the composer and pianist Moscheles, and the violinist Franz Clement, to whom Beethoven's Violin Concerto was dedicated. Clement's extraordinary ability to make a piano score of Haydn's *Seasons* after hearing it only a few times (with just the help of the libretto), so amazed Weber that he engaged Clement as leader of the Prague orchestra. With Salieri, however, he refused to make friends, aware of the composer's hatred for his beloved Mozart.

For Weber, it was a whirlwind of meetings, auditions, concert-going, scores to be copied and collected, and the important business of socialising. Small wonder, then, that when he came to arrange a concert of his own in Vienna on 25 April, his playing lacked its usual neatness and precision and the critics judged it to be inferior to that of such pianists as Hummel and Moscheles.

What had actually happened was that he had become ill before the concert. Afterwards, without any leave-taking, he hastened back to Prague, where he stayed alone in his rooms with a raging fever until Count Pachta chanced to visit him. Immediately, he was taken to the Count's home, where it was some three weeks before he recovered.

Weeks of intense activity followed. Weber's intention to reorganise the entire company, both orchestra and singers, had brought about such a storm of protest that he was obliged to dismiss more of the original company than at first envisaged. 'The orchestra is in rebellion', he wrote to Gottfried Weber on 21 May,

. . . and in the midst of all this worry, I have to correspond with all the new members to be engaged and draw up their contracts; rearrange and catalogue the disordered library; correct scores and describe scenery to the painters, costumes to the costumiers . . . I get up at six o'clock and am often at work until midnight. How happy I shall be when the machine begins to function.

In many ways, Weber had fortuitously timed his arrival in

Prague rather well. The city, which had been a quiet backwater, was beginning to teem with life. The Emperor of Austria had taken up his residence nearby, and Prague had been nominated as the venue for the coming abortive Peace Congress. Fugitives poured in from the scenes of war in Saxony and Prussia, including statesmen, diplomatists, political literati and their countless hangers-on. Neither was there any dearth of artists and intellectuals. Weber, although moving in the same circles as statesmen such as the Austrian commander-in-chief of the Allies' Grand Army of Bohemia, Prince Schwartzenberg, nevertheless paid little attention to the political ferment of the times. His hatred of the French invaders was real enough, but no record exists that it took any form other than that of a normal patriotic reaction.

By 12 August, the new operatic company was nearly completed, and Weber began the rehearsals of Spontini's *Fernand Cortez*, the first of 62 operas that he was to produce during his Prague intendancy. Some idea of his unremitting activity can be gauged from the fact that his hopes of giving two new operas every month were not infrequently improved upon; in both September and October 1813 he staged three.

Along with these exertions, Weber was unfortunate enough to get entangled with a thoroughly unscrupulous and scheming singer who sang light operatic parts with considerable success. She was married to a dancer in the company named Brunetti and, although the mother of five children, still retained her enviable figure and a reputation of being a mistress of all the finest arts of coquetry. Thrown together on a number of occasions, even during rehearsals in which she was not involved, Weber soon fell for the seductive Therese Brunetti with a passion that blinded him of all clear thought. So ensnared was he, that he even moved in with her and her acquiescent husband, oblivious to all entreaties from his friends. Once assured of her power over him, she played fast and loose with his feelings. Whatever the weather, he would willingly scour the town for ribbons or rings that she wanted, only to return to her and have them tossed aside disdainfully. His diary makes it clear that, in his subconscious, he knew she was worthless, but yet could not resist her. One day he writes: 'A fearful scene . . . The sweetest dream of my life is over.' On the next: 'This reconciliation has cleared the thunder from the air. Both of us felt better.' And then again, in November:

She does not love me. If she did, could she speak of her first love and all its cherished feelings with so much delight! Could she be so pitiless? No! My dream is over. I shall never know the happiness of being loved. I must for ever be alone! . . . I will do all I can to please her; but I must withdraw within myself, bury all my bitter feelings in my own heart, and work – work – work!

Work he certainly did. His efforts to bring efficiency and discipline to the opera company were almost superhuman.

Fernand Cortez was successfully produced on 9 September. Writing to Gänsbacher, Weber reports that it:

. . . went off admirably, and pleased, as much as anything can please, these cold beings. The orchestra and chorus did all that was possible, and I was very well satisfied.

In fact, one of the problems Weber had to deal with was the female chorus which, regretfully, had to be augmented by boys. Nevertheless, the consensus of opinion was that 'the freshly organised opera did the new *Kapellmeister* the greatest honour.'

All through the autumn, Weber persevered with his reorganisation of the company. There was no time for composition, even if he felt so inclined. Earlier, in March, he had completed two of his finest songs, 'Sind es Schmerzen' and 'Unbefangenheit', worked on his Clarinet Quintet for Bärmann (which he had begun in Switzerland), and transcribed the short violin piece *Andante e Rondo Ungarese* for his bassoonist friend, Brandt. But there was no major work on the horizon, like an opera. The reasons for this are many. Unlike Johann Poissl, who became a friend of Weber through Vogel, and was the first German composer to write his own libretti – mostly in Italianate style – Weber was seeking something new from writers with practical theatrical knowledge. With this end in view, Weber had sent Rochlitz an advertisement in March, couched in general terms, for inclusion in the *Allgemeine musikalische Zeitung*:

The undersigned wishes to acquire as soon as possible a good opera libretto for setting to music, and is prepared to pay a good price. He hereby invites any German poet prepared to undertake this work to submit a manuscript to the author of this advertisement, stating his terms; and he undertakes to return the manuscript to the poet, should it prove unsuitable to his purpose, without in any way misusing the copy.

Prague 12 March 1813

Carl Maria von Weber
Kapellmeister,
Director of the Opera of the *Königliches Böhnisches*

This was printed, though it would seem Weber received no response – certainly none that he found acceptable.

On 11 December, Caroline Brandt arrived in Prague and, on 1 January 1814, made her début in the title rôle of Isouard's *Cendrillon*, a part she had carried off to perfection in many of the capitals of Germany. The Prague author, Joseph Hanslick, father of the famous music critic Eduard Hanslick, was so moved by her performance as Cendrillon that he dedicated to her 'An Impromptu in Five Lines':

> *Für Dich war diese Dichtung nicht geschrieben,*
> *Sonst wär des Magus Rolle weggeblieben.*
> *Du brauchst den eignen Zauber nur zu üben,*
> *Und alle Herze fühlen sich getrieben,*
> *Dich, liebevolle zu lieben.*

Max Maria, in his biography of his mother, refers to:

. . . her exquisite form, her innocently coquettish grace, her sweet supple voice, her stage-sense and her powers of invention, which enabled her to dare much which others would have feared . . .

Caroline was born in 1794, and her early years were not unlike Weber's, roaming the land with her actress mother and singer-cum-violinist father, who had something of Franz Anton's quixotic nature. She made her stage début at the age of eight and, with her performance in the mime/speaking rôle of Silvana in 1810 at the age of 16, was already a seasoned actress.

After receiving the rare honour of winning a curtain-call for her performance as Cinderella, Weber introduced Brandt to the music-loving aristocracy of Prague – much to the consternation and jealousy of Therese Brunetti, with whom he was still entangled. But the end of the affair was in sight. When Therese ignored a gold watch he gave her as a birthday present, but gluttonously flung herself upon a dish of oysters (a costly delicacy in Prague), which he had ordered for her at the same time, Weber was disgusted. His eyes were finally opened, and the affair was brought to an end when Therese told him that she and her husband had been offered an apartment in the house of another of her lovers, a rich banker named Calina. She had advised Caroline to do likewise with another wealthy banker, Kleinwächter. Fortunately for Weber, Caroline took no notice of this counselling and his growing affection for her began to be reciprocated.

On 15 January 1814, Weber, for his first benefit night, chose *Don Giovanni* and cast Caroline as Zerlina, a rôle that established her in the eyes of the public. Max Maria tells us: 'From day to day she delighted Weber more and more, not only by her talent but by her never-failing modesty, her amiability towards her jealous colleagues, and her willingness in all.'

He could not fail to see the contrast between the life-styles of the two women. Caroline, after all, lived a secluded existence with her mother, impervious to all the advances of Prague's 'men about town'. One day, whilst talking to him on stage, Caroline was flung to the ground and injured by some falling scenery. Weber escorted her home, and thus began a series of visits of which her mother and, later, her father and brother, freely approved. Therese, realising Weber's deep affection for Caroline, promptly made a bid to drive a wedge between them and lure Weber back into the net, even though she had long since wearied of him. Caught in the middle of this difficult situation, Weber was further depressed to learn of the death of his old master, Vogler, on 6 May. 'Peace be to his ashes! I have much to thank him for, and he has always shown me the most sincere affection', he wrote in his diary. Weber's own health was fast deteriorating, so, at the beginning of July, he passed over the conductorship to the violinist, Clement, and left, with relief, on his three-month holiday.

In a frank letter to Gänsbacher from the spa of Liebwerda, where he was taking the waters, he declares:

. . . perhaps you will scarcely believe me when I say that I left Prague with a heavy heart, but you will readily understand why, when I tell you that I left there a beloved being who might make me happy and joyful, and it seems to me that she loves me truly. Do not be afraid, however, that I am blind and that my past experiences have not made me careful and distrustful, but I intend to find out whether she is genuine, and this three-month absence should put the matter to the test. But I go rambling on as if you knew all about it. The lady is Caroline Brandt, whom I love with all my heart, and every day I pray that God will make her a little better than other women.

Their separation did not, however, preclude an exchange of letters, of which only Weber's have been preserved. Caroline, aware of the termination of the Brunetti liaison, must, nevertheless, have been filled with doubts and fears, and not a little overwhelmed by the ardent protestations of love on Weber's side. Their deepening mutual involvement was only slowly, and hazardously, to reach the desired end – marriage.

After three weeks in Liebwerda, Weber travelled on to Berlin, arriving there on 3 August. Here, everything had changed since his last visit. Gone was the oppressive atmosphere of a city weighed down by the occupation of a foreign power. Now there was an aura of tense excitement and jubilation. Through their own efforts, the German people had rid the Fatherland of Napoleon's

A later painting of Caroline von Weber (née Brandt), painted by her son Alexander von Weber.

forces, which had been pushed back to Paris; Berlin, like the rest of Germany, was free, and the mighty Napoleon, from an empire larger than that of Augustus, was shortly to be exiled to the tiny island of Elba.

On the night he arrived, Weber found that most of his musical friends, including Lichtenstein, were attending a performance at the *Singakademie*, and was touched when the words 'Weber is here' ran through the auditorium. On 7 August, the King returned to Berlin and the city was given over to wild patriotic celebrations. With the town brilliantly illuminated, Weber joined the throng of sightseers and, at one moment, was nearly jostled under an advancing carriage. Letting out a cry, Weber recognised inside the poet Tieck, who, dragging Weber to safety, shouted triumphantly 'Now I understand the reason for the illuminations and what brings us to Berlin!'

82

The *Singakademie* in Berlin.

Patriotic celebrations.

Away from his official responsibilities, Weber found a new desire to compose. He writes:

I discover, to my joy, that a host of musical ideas are teeming in my head. I must labour hard to execute all my intentions; and yet I live in such a stormy restless whirl, that I am never satisfied with my own doings.

As things turned out, little was done in the way of composition during his stay in Berlin. Brentano, who was there at the time, enthused about the mediaeval legend of *Tannhäuser* but, though Weber was excited by its musical possibilities, nothing was to come of the idea.

Weber's only public concert in Berlin, which had been frequently postponed, eventually took place on 26 August to an enthusiastic audience. Besides playing his Piano Concerto in E flat, his inventive improvisation skills were particularly well received. There was also a performance of *Silvana*, which was well attended, but little to the taste of the audience who, in these stirring times, wanted stronger fare. Nevertheless it had been worthwhile. Many members of the company and the orchestra secretly pressed Weber's hand and murmured that they wanted him to stay. He was led to believe that when the present Intendant of the opera, the aged Iffland (who had snubbed Weber in the past) died, he might well be considered for the post – '. . . great things are to be done – we want you, and must have you.' Meanwhile, immediately after the performance, Weber left the city in a torrent of rain.

After a short stay in Leipzig, he returned once more to Weimar, where he found a letter from Liebich pressing for his return to Prague, as Clement was proving to be a bad conductor. However, Weber decided he must have all the leave to which he was entitled and continued on his way to Gotha and the nearby castle of Gräfen-Tonna, where his friend Duke Emil was taking the waters. To Caroline he writes:

The wonderful old castle where I sit in a bare room with rattling doors and windows gives me a certain pleasant sense of stillness and repose . . . In the midst of my throat and finger employments with the Duke, which one day occupied me twelve hours at a stretch, I have found time to arrange my papers, and compose.

The compositions were two songs, patriotic outpourings that were the beginnings of his *Leyer und Schwert* that finally occupied three volumes. Called 'Lützows wilde Jagd' and 'Schwertlied', they were to blaze a trail through Germany, and speed Weber to a new pinnacle of popularity. They were all songs set to verses of the young poet Theodor Körner, a fallen hero who had been killed the previous year in battle.

But Weber's time in Gotha was cut short by another pleading letter from Liebich, entreating him to return to Prague at once. This time there was no option; Weber returned to Prague on 25 September, a full two weeks earlier than his contract demanded. Although Liebich, in true impresario fashion, exaggerated the problems that had arisen, Weber was nevertheless required to exert his authority to get the theatre working smoothly again.

Theodor Körner.

Although delighted to see his beloved Caroline once more, some friction soon ensued when she heard about his *Leyer und Schwert* settings. Caroline was born in the Bonapartist city of Bonn, and regarded Napoleon as 'the greatest hero of his age'. She objected strongly to Weber's alignment with the national aspirations reflected in Körner's poetry. Another cause for rancour was Weber's insistence that, after their marriage, which he urged upon her, she should give up the stage for ever. To Lichtenstein, who had himself become engaged, Weber wrote despairingly:

Heaven grant you a good wife who will make you happy . . . all my fondest hopes for this diminish day by day . . . I love her with all my heart, but if there is no sincerity in her feelings, the last chord of my whole life has been struck. I live on and perhaps will marry, but love and trust again – nevermore!

Another matter of a different nature arose to complicate his life. Iffland, the Intendant of the Berlin court theatre had at last died, and Count Brühl, who succeeded him, immediately offered Weber the post of Chief Conductor, about which so many hints had been dropped earlier. Although Weber considered the offer, in the end he declined it, preferring to remain in Prague, staging new productions.

One of the most outstanding of these was the staging of *Fidelio* on 24 November which, alas, met with indifference. 14 rehearsals had been lavished on it (an exceptional number for those days) and Weber, angry at its reception, expressed his disgust in a letter to Gänsbacher:

I performed Beethoven's *Fidelio* which went to perfection; what wonderful things there are in that music, but they don't understand it. It is enough to drive me mad!

Despairing of the artistic acumen of Prague audiences, it is hardly surprising that Weber should have turned to his beloved Caroline for solace. Persisting in his endeavours to get her to marry him, he undertook the management of her accounts with scrupulous attention and, according to Max Maria, took on all the business of her mother as well. In January 1815 he went a little too far when he let it be known that, in order to increase the receipts for Caroline's benefit performance of Cinderella, he himself would sell the tickets at the box office! The gossip and scandal-mongers had a field day when he actually remained there the whole day, trying, with his charming manner, to obtain the highest possible price for the tickets. Caroline was furious at being ridiculed by this indiscretion, and demanded time for further reflection before agreeing to marry him. Weber threatened to leave Prague but, in fact, resorted to another bout of hard work.

Towards the end of January, Bärmann's famous rival clarinet-tist, Hermstedt, arrived in Prague. Weber's diary for 4 February records that he composed a *Savoyisches Lied* and a Clarinet Concerto for Hermstedt, and Max Maria writes that Weber finished the two new works in time to play them with Hermstedt at the latter's second concert, but neither work has come to light.

During this period too, Caspar and Anton Fürstenau – father and son virtuoso flautists – were present in Prague. Weber composed for them a *Schöfen Klage*, which in all probability eventually became the Andante of the Trio for piano, flute and cello, which was composed in 1819 and dedicated to his Prague cellist friend Dr Jung.

Chapter 14

Problems with Caroline

After these compositions, Weber wrote little else in the first half of 1815. For a performance of Méhul's *Helena* on 4 January he interpolated an aria specially written for Therese Grünbaum's benefit night. (The practice of inserting a new aria into somebody else's opera was quite common at that time, and was something that Weber did on a number of occasions, though one gathers that he did not really approve of it.) There was also one of his best sets of variations for piano on a Russian theme, *Schöne Minka*.

As the year progressed, Weber had further domestic problems; most importantly his relations with Caroline suffered a setback. This time there appears to have been little foundation for her fit of jealousy, which centred round a newly-engaged actress called Christine Böhler, towards whom she falsely accused Weber of giving undue attention. Caroline now urged on Weber the very step against which she had once protested with so many tears and entreaties, namely that one of them must leave Prague. Weber, in a very dejected state of mind, decided to anticipate his leave of absence by a month and left Prague for Munich on 6 June. Their relationship was now at a critical stage: Caroline obsessed with doubts and uncertainties about taking the final step and marrying him, Weber fearful that he might lose her altogether. Yet, as had happened before, they were soon exchanging letters. In his biography Max Maria states:

It was one of the characteristics of Weber's affectionate and sympathetic nature that, when separated from those he loved, he strove by every means to connect them as intimately as possible in his daily life. He had parted from his beloved 'more in sorrow than in anger'; and some of the strongest evidence of this peculiar characteristic may be found in the pains he took in his letters to Caroline to describe to her every detail of the chamber in which he was lodged, and thus to associate her with every object around him. 'I am so charmed to find', he wrote to her, 'that we generally write to each other on the same day.' (In fact, their letters frequently crossed.) 'It is so pleasant to think that at the same moment as

Biedermeier-style living room c.1820.

myself, perhaps, you are occupied at your well-known table. In future let me know the very hour, as well as the day, on which you write. But you cannot tell where I am sitting. Call your fancy to aid, whilst I make you a plan of the little room I occupy.' There follows a plan of the chamber with every article of furniture marked with scrupulous exactitude. 'You see', he continues, 'that when I want to roam up and down in my den, I must use considerable adroitness in winding in and out, so as not to upset my furniture. Would that I could give you as accurate a picture of my whole soul! You alone occupy it entirely.'

Weber arrived in Munich on 18 June. On the same day the Battle of Waterloo was fought outside Brussels, with Allied forces, including British and Prussian troops, opposing the advancing armies of Napoleon. When news of Wellington's victory reached Munich, the city, as though by magic, took on an air of carnival, with illuminations, fireworks and salvos of cannon, all hastily improvised. The nightmare for Germany, of further invasion by the French, was suddenly removed. Weber, along with the exuberant crowds, entered the *Michaeliskirche* for a thanksgiving service. Whilst listening to the ringing tones of the Te Deum, the idea of a splendid Cantata of Victory floated before his mind. On leaving the church, he happened to meet the actor and poet Johann Wohlbrück, and, seizing his arm, told him of his inspiration. By 2 August, Wohlbrück's text *Kampf und Sieg* was in Weber's hands, but the composition was slow in materialising. This was partly due to the socialising he was expected to do, but mostly because of the continuing unsettled state of his mind. In a letter to Caroline, he confesses that '. . . sometimes I think that all power of productiveness is lost to me for ever'. The Cantata, *Kampf und Sieg* (J.190) for soloists, chorus and orchestra was not to be completed until December.

Meanwhile, whilst staying with Bärmann during the summer, Weber gave a number of concerts. Then, on 25 August, he finally completed his Clarinet Quintet, on which he had been working spasmodically since 1811. Bärmann performed it for the first time the following day to a capacity audience that included royalty. This bubble of success was soon burst, however, by a letter he received from Caroline on 3 September explaining that, after a lot of thought, 'she was convinced that it was for the happiness of them both' that their association should end.

Weber returned to Prague on 7 September in a miserable state, which turned to wild agitation when he saw Caroline that very night, singing her famous rôle of Cendrillon. His old friend Gänsbacher, who was then in Prague, offered some comfort to the distraught lover, but Weber's duties naturally brought him into frequent contact with the 'woman he had lost, but still loved so fondly.' Nevertheless, he decided to try to put a brave face on it. Caroline, for her part, confides Max Maria, 'found it more difficult to hide her feelings'. The real affection she had for Weber burst forth again at the sight of him. Then, one fine autumn afternoon, Weber and his friend Gänsbacher accepted an invitation from Liebich to visit his new house just outside the city. There they found a large party assembled, with the socially élite of Prague mingling with the artists of the theatre. Here, at last, the lovers were finally reconciled and their mutual happiness restored.

Fired with a new vigour, Weber continued composing the Cantata *Kampf und Sieg*. To Gottfried he had written already, telling him that he would

. . . send the score to all the Sovereigns. The local English Ambassador is sending it to the Prince Regent, and seeing to an English translation. You can imagine how much this kind of work, which justifies my career in the world, occupies me day and night, and THANK GOD! During the past few days that I've been thinking about it, I've been feeling the return of my powers and the hope that I may still do something useful in the world.

Apart from the Cantata, Weber completed a number of minor occasional pieces at this time.

Aware that he must perform *Kampf und Sieg* before the excitement of the past victories evaporated, Weber at last had the Cantata ready for performance on 22 December. His 'evil star' was at work again, however, inflicting appalling weather on the night of the performance. Those who braved the storms were cold and disgruntled. Weber's valuable idea of having the poem declaimed first, to enable fuller comprehension of the work, made no impact at all. The performance itself was a different matter, with the audience quickly growing enthusiastic. Max Maria writes:

The success which attended the efforts of the master to combine a musical picture of great events with the stirring feelings those events had aroused, was recognised at once. Equally applauded by the more cultivated section of the audience was the text, and the skill with which the composer had avoided all the customary effects of the clash of arms, the thunder of the cannon, the cries of the wounded, and such commonplace resources, whilst bestowing a general dramatic effect, which swept on victoriously. The introduction of the various national airs was declared to be as clever as it was effective. At the conclusion, General Nostitz, who had played a decisive rôle in the battle of Leipzig, walked up to Weber and said, in allusion to Beethoven's *Wellington's Victory* which had recently been performed, 'In Beethoven's music boys play at soldiers; in yours sir, we have heard the voices of nations.'

The success of *Kampf und Sieg* did little to persuade Weber that he wished to stay on in Prague. He had worked extremely hard to raise the standard of opera production overall and, to a great extent, he had succeeded: now he felt that Prague was musically limited and that his career was being hampered. When Liebich passed on to him a formal complaint from the governing body of the theatre 'to the effect', writes Weber, in a letter to Gänsbacher, 'that for the last three years [he'd] done nothing for the opera', Weber resolved to leave Prague 'at all costs'.

His desire to depart had a powerful effect on Caroline's mind. Seeking to relieve his loneliness, she persuaded her mother to let him lodge in her house. His health soon improved and his spirits revived. Nevertheless, in the Easter of 1816, Weber submitted his resignation, to take effect from the autumn. The only music he wrote during this period was the orchestral *Tedesco* (J.191) and some songs.

In the meantime, Weber had sent *Kampf und Sieg* to the King of Prussia, requesting his permission to perform it at the Opera House in Berlin on the anniversary of Waterloo, for the benefit of invalided soldiers. On permission being granted, he set out for that city on 5 June. Passing through Dresden, Weber was presented with a gold snuffbox by the King's equerry, Count Heinrich Vitzthum in recognition of the gift of the score. Weber reached Berlin and the Beer family's house on 9 August. A performance of the Cantata met with success, and, much to Weber's joy, Brühl arranged for Caroline to make some 'star' appearances in Berlin. She was engaged to appear in six different rôles at an exceptionally high salary: 'You ought to be pleased with your commissioner', wrote the happy lover, 'and be aware you owe him several good extra kisses on his return.'

During his time in Berlin, Weber again met E.T.A. Hoffmann, who gave him a copy of his recently published book, *Die Elixiere des Teufels*. This book, together with the same author's *Phantasie-stücke in Callots Manier*, fascinated Weber, with its cultivation of the more grotesque aspects of Romanticism. Hoffmann's opera *Undine*, which was to have a marked influence on Weber's *Der Freischütz*, was given its first performance less than a month after Weber's departure for Carlsbad on 9 July.

Apart from wishing to take the waters in Carlsbad for his rheumatism, it seems that Weber had been requested to have a further meeting with the King's equerry Count Vitzthum, on the pretext of discussing the engagement of a tenor singer. Vitzthum, however, had recently been appointed the Intendant of the Royal Theatre in Dresden, where he hoped to establish a German Opera. Weber struck him as the right man for the job of *Kapellmeister*, and, in a letter to his brother, Vitzthum dwelt on Weber's talent in that sphere.

Negotiations started, but nothing was firmly settled. There is no doubt, though, that Weber, disillusioned with Prague, found the idea attractive.

Weber returned to Prague on 18 July. 'Papa' Liebich, as he was affectionately called, was now gravely ill and permanently confined to his bed. With renewed energy, Weber was, as ever, adventurous in the operas he chose to stage. On 1 September, Spohr's *Faust* was performed. Spohr's idea of using the overture to crystallise the feelings and events of the whole opera was not lost on Weber, who followed this scheme in all his later operas.

Weber worked relentlessly to leave everything in meticulous order for his successor, Joseph Triebensee. As proof of his generous nature, he left him a detailed account of all aspects of his job, down to the characteristics of each artist, which was by no means required of him. When, on 7 October, Weber finally relinquished his post, Max Maria recounts:

. . . the whole body of the company, from orchestra and stage, from leading singers and first tragedians to carpenters, thronged round his carriage, with broken voices and tears in their eyes, to bid him farewell.

But this time he was not alone. Caroline, along with her mother, travelled with him, to take up the choice engagements he had procured for her in Berlin.

Over the last few months, Caroline had been wavering over Weber's offer of marriage. But, on seeing how warmly he was welcomed in Berlin, and how esteemed he was there, her feelings began to change. According to Max Maria:

One evening, on returning from a party where the greatest homage had been done him, Weber begged permission to announce their engagement, and both ladies welcomed with open arms the offer, which, just a few months earlier, they had hesitated to accept.

Weber was overjoyed, and after Caroline left Berlin to fulfil certain engagements in Dresden, he began composing again. In a few weeks he wrote two of his most charming songs, 'Die gefängenen Sänger' and 'Die freien Sänger', completed his Piano Sonata in A flat and composed the *Grand Due Concertant* for clarinet and piano.

Meanwhile, Count Vitzthum was busy negotiating the terms for Weber's appointment as *Kapellmeister* to the German Opera at Dresden. Although delaying tactics were employed at first by Cabinet Minister Count Einsiedel, on the grounds that 'all arrangements for a German Opera were in too crude a state to

Count Einsiedel.

admit any thought of such appointments', Vitzthum was too clever a character to be fobbed off.

On Christmas morning 1816, he sent Weber a letter. Not daring to open it at first, the composer finally 'plucked up courage', and, as he wrote later in a letter to Caroline:

It was joy! So round I went to all my friends, who laughed, and made the new Royal *Kapellmeister* the most reverential bows. I must dress myself in true court style. Perhaps I ought to wear a pigtail to please the Dresdeners! What do you think? I ought to have an extra kiss from you for this good news.

Chapter 15

Dresden

Weber assumed his new post at the Dresden Theatre on 13 January 1817. It took him a little while to settle in, but his circle of friends and acquaintances increased daily. Some people, Max Maria tells us, received the celebrated newcomer with real delight, while 'others, as yet uncertain how far the stranger might stand in favour in high quarters, were smooth and bland, and made sweet faces, and held themselves ready to spin the thread of friendship to any extent, or snap it off altogether, according to future circumstances.'

There were soon problems, however, as the Dresden musical public was divided into two strongly antagonistic musical camps.

On the one hand, there were those who favoured Italian music; this group was very powerful as it included the royal family and much of the local aristocracy. On the other, there were those who felt the need for a fully German opera; with very few exceptions, members of this group tended to come from the middle and lower classes of the city.

At this time, Dresden was, even by the standards of the period, a remarkably conservative place. At the top of the hierarchy was the royal family and the court; they ruled with a kind of benevolent absolution, requiring the populace to follow their guidance obediently and unquestioningly. As Max Maria records in his trenchant way, there was hardly any trade in the town, and no university to encourage individuality of thinking; all that was required of the people was a blind confidence in the patriarchal system of government. Max Maria was particularly appalled by the impoverished culture of the Saxon nobility:

Instead of endeavouring to reassert the position which it had lost after the partition of the country, by raising its own intellectual standard and cultivating the fine arts . . . it shut itself up in its own narrow circle in which it lived, intermarried, vegetated and died. Little as it understood the sense of the word 'sociability', it designated itself by the exclusive

94

term 'society'. It prescribed every active experience of intellect as 'vulgar'. It brought up its *Fräulein* and its *Junker* to confine their views to their own petty sphere; the truest elements of cultivation for the nobleman – travel, observation, comparison, and mixing with other classes, it looked upon with horror. All tendencies towards improvement or novelty were repudiated by it as symptoms of unpatriotic feeling. At the same time, despite this carefully cultivated narrowness of ideas, and despite its want of manner and morality, the Saxon nobility pretended, as its especial right and privilege, to all the first and most important posts at court, to all distinctions in the government or the army, to all that could help its needs and fill its pockets. Under the patriarchal government of the day every post was dependent on the direct will of the sovereign. From the purple and gold of the throne alone, then, could the nobility, in the position it had assumed, derive any brilliancy.

Thus, at the beginning of the present century, there was no tradition with which to inspire the Dresdeners to any show of energy, or to bestow on them any distinctive character.

King Friedrich August was respected by his Saxon people (they nicknamed him 'The Just'), and his comings and goings were a source of perpetual fascination to them. As late as 1820, the royal family adhered to the costume and formal trappings of absolutist monarchs, dressing themselves and behaving as they might well have done over two hundred years earlier. Dresdeners crowded the passages and galleries of the court and watched with reverence as the royal family moved itself into position with the precision of clockwork. According to a somewhat incredulous contemporary report:

The gentlemen were all in antiquated uniforms and obsolete court-dresses, with powdered wigs, and long pigtails hanging down their backs; the ladies, similarly, wore powdered head-dresses – and this in the year 1820! When the court went to church, on Sundays and high holidays, at eleven o'clock, on the first stroke of the hour, the royal procession began its march through the hanging-passage, leading from the palace; at the very moment of the last stroke every person sat down, and the service began. The royal family, with their wretched wrinkled faces, all miserably ugly, looked, behind their glazed gallery, like a row of mummies in glass cases. Thus, also, on their visits to the theatre, where the representations began at six precisely, a similar procession started on the stroke of the hour; on the last of these, the King entered the box. The audience rose, and only sat down again when all the court was seated. And never was a single departure made from this ceremonial by one second through long years.

When, in 1697, King Friedrich August the Strong had turned Catholic, Rome seized the opportunity to assert itself culturally and politically in Saxony. An Italian colony was founded in

95

Dresden; at one end of the social spectrum it included the architects and labourers brought from Italy to build Dresden's new Catholic churches; at the other, it included highly cultured and ambitious men whose main concern was to get their hands on positions of power and influence. As a result of their efforts, Italian taste still dominated in all walks of life: anything else was considered 'mere barbarism'. As Max Maria put it:

Polite, elegant and supple, and at the same time artful and unscrupulous as they were, they soon persuaded the compliant Germans that only in Italy was there a perfect civilisation; all that was refined, distinguished, and tasteful was Italian. All who stood in any relation, however distant, to the court, believed it their duty to show an exclusive devotion to Italian art. In all the fine arts, but more especially in music, Italian taste was the only one deemed admissible in good society. A choir had been founded upon the Italian model; and Italian opera was the exclusive opera of the court. Italian directors of the court music, Italian composers, Italian singers became the sole arbiters of musical taste . . . Imbued, as the public was, with the notion that royal taste must necessarily be met with equal loyal admiration, it would have been considered ridiculously presumptuous to imagine that any other nation could contest the palm, on the great course of musical art, with the Italians.

Since the prevailing taste amongst the aristocracy was for Italian opera, any suggestion that there might be some value in German opera was not taken seriously. The Italians had all the advantages: their establishment had been set up over a century earlier; they had the best theatres, the best performers, the best librettists. By comparison, German opera seemed a very unsophisticated affair, to be associated with troupes of travelling players who performed in makeshift theatres for a few days and then moved on.

Originally, Italian opera in Dresden had been reserved exclusively for the aristocracy. But, as the court found itself getting further and further into debt as a result of massive military expenditure, Friedrich August decided to economise by opening the doors of his court theatre to the public.

The King himself never ventured into the public streets of Dresden, and his voice had never been heard by his people. The process of governing and making decisions was done by the King's ministers, chief among them being Count Einsiedel, a man of some refinement; but a bureaucratic formalist, terrified of any sign of individuality amongst his staff. He had never travelled, and Max Maria likened him to a man who had looked at his house only from within, and knew nothing of the cracks on the outside, through which wind and rain could penetrate. No Saxon could be a good patriot, according to Einsiedel, if he imbibed ideas from places outside Dresden.

Needless-to-say, Einsiedel was one of the staunchest supporters of the traditional Italian Opera, and, as a result, extremely hostile to the idea of establishing a German Opera. Italian opera, by its very nature, helped bolster the mystique of the court, but German opera, with its readily-understood narrative and familiar everyday subject matter, could be used to subvert the traditional political order.

In Einsiedel's eyes, Weber had already blotted his copybook before he arrived in Dresden, by writing *Leyer und Schwert*, songs of triumph over the defeated Napoleon. King Friedrich August was a devoted ally and supporter of Napoleon, and Einsiedel was fond of reminding the King that his new court composer was a potential subversive.

When the Russians had occupied Dresden in 1814, they had entirely remodelled the system of the Dresden Theatre, reorganising the administration, and even mooting the idea of establishing a German Opera. But nothing was done about this until the King returned in 1815 and appointed Count Heinrich Vitzthum to be Director of the Dresden Theatre and to oversee the matter.

There was no love lost between Vitzthum and Einsiedel, and, in order to put both Vitzthum and Weber in their places, Einsiedel deliberately showed a marked preference for Francesco Morlacchi, the *Kapellmeister* of the Italian Opera.

Morlacchi was two years older than Weber, and, after beginning life as a violinist in Italy, he had, in 1807, begun another career as an opera composer. After coming to Dresden, he quickly became a favourite of the King and, as a result, of Einsiedel. Max Maria describes him fairly, noting that although he was well-versed in the technicalities of his art, he lacked the strength of character to make a good conductor. He also says that:

As a man, he was a true pupil of the Jesuits, under whom he had studied, delighting in intrigue and full of unnecessary *finesse*. During all the years he had resided in Germany, he had deliberately never learned the language, in order to have excuses for any misunderstandings it was his wish to make. His want of manliness, his slyness and subserviency rendered him antipathetical to Count Vitzthum.

Morlacchi was to make a lot of trouble for Weber during his years in Dresden, by sabotaging his efforts in one way or another, or by having his workload increased to unreasonable proportions. One of the most depressing situations that Weber would find himself in, was that of having his compositions rejected by the court in favour of Morlacchi's. But there were two men other than Vitzthum who sided with Weber.

One was the former director of the Dresden Theatre, Franz

Italian composer Francesco
Morlacchi.

Seconda, who at one time had been imprisoned by the Russians as
a French spy, and, as Max Maria tells us, was 'senile or insolent,
according to whether those he addressed were supposed to be in
favour or disfavour'. The other was the great Italian baritone,
Luigi Bassi, for whom Mozart had written the rôle of Don
Giovanni. Now 50, and with his singing voice gone, Bassi was no
longer able to perform, but Morlacchi had decided to make use of
his experience by appointing him to the post of stage manager of
the Italian Opera. Both he and Seconda were to prove loyal
advocates for Weber in his endeavours to succeed with mounting
German opera.

Shortly after arriving in Dresden, Weber found lodgings in the
Italian sector. He had his piano installed, laid carpets on all the
floors – with his nervous disposition, Weber could not stand the
sound of feet on bare boards – and hired a manservant, as was
necessary to the dignity of his new position. We know all this
because Weber was very proud of his new home, and described
every nook and cranny of it in his letters to Caroline.

But, although Weber may have been delighted by his living
quarters, he found the theatre distinctly less satisfactory. The

auditorium had excellent acoustics, but the backstage facilities were abysmal.

Vitzthum had, over the years, tried to persuade the King to enlarge the theatre or even to build a new one, but in the end he had been forced to compromise by using an already existing theatre on the Linckesche Bad, in the public gardens across the River Elbe.

Weber's first visitor was Morlacchi, who welcomed him over-ostentatiously. As the Italian spoke no German, and only a little French, conversation between the two men was difficult and Weber quickly realised that he was at a disadvantage. So he resolved to learn Italian and, with his facility for languages, quickly mastered it.

He was also visited by Bassi, who wasted no time in telling him that the position he held in Dresden was inferior to that of Morlacchi. The title of Weber's appointment was *Musikdirektor*, whilst Morlacchi's post with the Italian Opera was the superior one of *Königlich Kapellmeister*. Weber had accepted his position in the belief that he was to be on an equal footing with Morlacchi. 'No such thing', cried Bassi in a passion: 'your diploma is made out as "Director of the German Opera", not *Kapellmeister*. I have seen it.' Weber was furious. He threatened to resign, and it was only after Vitzthum had taken the matter to the King, that he eventually achieved equal status with Morlacchi. Even then, this only came about after the success of his first production in Dresden, Méhul's *Joseph in Egypt* on 30 January. Méhul's opera had first been given in Paris in 1807 and was later performed all over Europe. Weber admired it immensely, and his ideas about it give credence to the fact that the rise of German opera stemmed more from the example of the French school than anywhere else.

Weber's commitment to staging operas extended to all aspects of the performance, not just the music. He spent many hours in the royal library studying books on Egypt, so that he could advise the dressmakers and scenery designers. He would leap onto the stage in the middle of a rehearsal to regroup the chorus and tell them where to stand. Then he would leap back into the pit and correct mistakes in the orchestra.

In a newspaper article 'To the Art-loving Citizens of Dresden', which Weber wrote on taking up his appointment, he sought to underline the German predicament vis-à-vis opera:

No people has been so slow and so uncertain as the Germans in determining its own specific art forms. Both the Italians and the French have evolved a form of opera in which they move freely and naturally. This is not true of the Germans, whose peculiarity it has been to adopt what seems best in other schools, after much study and steady development; but the matter goes deeper with them. Whereas other nations concern themselves chiefly with the sensuous satisfaction of isolated moments, the German demands a self-sufficient work of art, in which all the parts make up a beautiful and unified whole.

Dresden 'society' was shocked that a court *Kapellmeister* – a salaried member of the King's staff – should have stooped so low as to write a newspaper article. In a letter to Caroline, Weber confesses that:

My article has created a great sensation – petrification and terror on the one hand, pleasure and respect on the other. What the hell! The good ones of the earth begin to love me, and the bad ones to fear me.

Before the opening of the German Opera, the King said, as he entered his box, 'If the show goes well, Weber will deserve all the credit.' And it did, in fact, succeed beyond all expectations. The King had a good ear, and he was prone to cough impatiently when anything displeased him, but on this occasion never once did he emit the ominous sound!

That Weber had achieved such a success, with a new kind of work and in the space of 18 days, was incredible. After all, his troupe of singers, including Italians, were inexperienced in such a field. Weber's reputation grew significantly, not only in court, but amongst the chorus and orchestra, who had suffered under the rather lax supervision of their former conductor.

Weber's relations with the orchestra had not always gone so smoothly. Soon after he arrived, Weber took his players aback by telling them: 'I expect total obedience. I shall be just, but pitilessly severe with all who need severity, myself among the number.' Such an outburst had never been heard before by any of the company, as Max Maria records:

For many generations, gentle wishes, not commands, had been the order of the day. At first all stood aghast and dumb. On leaving the theatre, at least two-thirds of the company declared themselves against the 'impertinent young musical director'. The members of the instrumental department were more than indignant. Never had even the most famous of *Kapellmeisters* thus dared to address the celebrated orchestra. And yet – such miracles will truth work – in a short time, some of the bitterest enemies of the hour became Weber's staunchest friends, supporters and admirers.

Newspaper reports on the production of Méhul's opera were laudatory, with the exception of one by an outspoken lady called Therese aus dem Winkel. She, like Weber, was a member of the 'Poets' Tea Society', a quaintly-named literary society which

100

frequently met in private houses to declaim and discuss new work. She wasted no time in publishing an article vilifying German opera, and contrasting it unfavourably with the Italian.

Nevertheless, Weber made many well-connected friends at the 'Poets' Tea Society', who were later to be of considerable importance to him. The president was Arthur von Nordstern (the pseudonym of the Minister Nostiz), one of the King's most liberal ministers, an opponent of Count Einsiedel and a man to whom Weber was devoted. It was also at one of the Society's meetings that he renewed his acquaintance with the poet Friedrich Kind, who would often read, in a creaking voice, passages from his latest works. Discerning a dramatic spirit pervading Kind's poetry, Weber managed on one occasion to leave the house with him, and, during a brief walk, talked him into writing an opera libretto. Many subjects were discussed, until suddenly the composer remembered how his friend Alexander von Dusch had grown so excited over the legend of *Der Freischütz*. Kind knew the story too, and the two men quickly became inspired by the subject.

In a letter to Caroline in February 1817 Weber announced:

The poet Friedrich Kind, librettist for *Der Freischütz*.

Friedrich Kind is going to begin an opera book for me this very day. The subject is admirable, interesting and horribly exciting. Do you know the old national legend of *Der Freischütz*?

Within a week, with the words of the first act completed and lying on his desk, Weber followed with another letter:

Kind hopes to have the whole thing ready in a fortnight. Well! It's remarkable stuff; the devil himself turns up in it. He appears as the Black Huntsman, and bullets are made in a ravine at midnight, with spectral appearances all around. Haven't I made your flesh creep?

Kind was true to his word. By the beginning of March, the whole book of *Der Freischütz* was in Weber's hands, and, after a little negotiation, Weber bought out the rights for 30 ducats.

He had very little time to compose the music, however, as his administrative obligations were extremely demanding. Much of his time was spent reorganising the management of the opera house, setting up a library there and reorganising the chorus.

Weber's plans were very ambitious. But permission to put them into effect had to be wrung from Count Einsiedel, who – needless-to-say – did all he could to slow them down.

And what little time Weber did have for composing, he spent on ephemeral things, such as incidental music for a Berlin production by Count Brühl – after all, a good friend and patron cannot be refused.

Despite all his commitments, Weber managed to find time to make his house worthy to receive his bride. He expected to have his appointment – initially only a year's contract – extended for life; then he would be in a position to provide the material security needed for marriage. In his daily letters to Caroline he details all his purchases – chairs, crockery, knives, pails, brooms, mustard pots and much else besides. 'Oh how my soul yearns', he wrote to his intended, 'for the moment when I can lead you into the sweet nest which will be yours, and, with your head upon my breast, I can whisper to you, "This is thy little kingdom, my own queen." '

Weber was obviously missing Caroline, but he did manage to get to Prague on one occasion to see her. As part of his duties, he had to engage singers, and, as the Prague Theatre had recently gone bankrupt, there were a lot of singers in the city anxious to find work.

So he set off in high spirits, invigorated by the idea of seeing his beloved once again. But his happiness was to be short-lived. On arriving in Prague, he was told that the bank which he used had become insolvent, and was going to be wound-up. Not only were Weber's own savings in this bank, but those of Caroline too.

'Courage!', he wrote in his diary, 'Heaven has helped me this far. It will help again, I trust to its mercy.' Weber managed to find enough money from other sources to replace Caroline's savings, and he never told her of the incident.

Apart from this, things went well in Prague – a production of *Silvana* was enthusiastically received, and Weber engaged the singer he required.

On returning to Dresden, he introduced a novelty into the theatre: he began to conduct with a baton. Traditionally, the conductor had sat at the piano, accompanying the orchestra, and had only marked time in difficult passages with a wave of the hand. The new method went down badly. Weber argued that, although the old system might be good enough for Italian opera, German music required more influence and input from the conductor.

Every innovation that Weber tried to make was greeted with hostility, and, as a result, he gave careful consideration to a letter from Count Brühl, inviting him to become *Kapellmeister* at the Berlin Opera.

The offer was tempting – it was a permanent post, whereas the Dresden contract was only for a year. But Weber was undecided, hoping, perhaps, that his situation at Dresden would improve, and in the end things turned out in a way that no-one could have predicted. On 31 July 1817, the Berlin theatre was burned to the ground, and, as a result, the King of Russia decided not to fill the vacancy after all.

So Weber stayed on in Dresden, and turned his attention to *Der Freischütz*. 'The great work before me terrifies me sometimes', he wrote to Caroline, 'and, with all the labours of my office, my correspondence and my conducting duties, how can I ever hope to complete it?'

The distractions Weber faced were immense. Social obligations, as well as professional ones, robbed him of time he would far rather have spent on *Der Freischütz*. In addition, Morlacchi went on leave of absence, leaving Weber to conduct all the church music and supervise all the domestic music-making in the royal court. Particularly tiresome was the so-called 'Table Music', which, following the strictest old-fashioned court etiquette, had to be conducted in full dress by the *Kapellmeister* himself, amidst the clattering of plates and glasses and the chatter of the diners.

Meanwhile, work continued on Weber's house, in preparation for married life. Much of *Der Freischütz* was written against a background of hammering and sawing. The house was in turmoil, and for many nights Weber had to sleep in the kitchen, working on his manuscript wherever he could find a flat surface.

Day by day, Weber's obligations to the court increased. He was asked to compose a cantata celebrating the marriage of Prince Max's daughter to the Grand Duke of Tuscany. A libretto in Italian had been prepared, and the original intention was that Morlacchi should compose the piece. But he was still away, so the task fell to Weber. He, like Count Vitzthum, thought that the wedding should be German in character, so a new libretto was commissioned, this time in German.

Things were going well, when Count Einsiedel took it into his head to interfere, saying that Italian was the only language that could possibly be contemplated for a royal festivity. So, in two weeks, Weber produced a setting of the Italian libretto, and had his cantata *L'Accoglienza* ready in time for the wedding.

Then, much to his horror, the royal wedding was postponed. Weber wanted to get away to Prague for his own marriage; instead he had to wait around in Dresden until the royal couple saw fit to marry. This they managed to do by proxy on 29 October 1817. Weber's cantata was enthusiastically received and the King himself sent Weber a diamond ring as a token of his satisfaction.

Afterwards, Weber set off for Prague as soon as he could. On 4 November 1817, after a morning of prayer and contemplation, he achieved his dearest wish by marrying Caroline in the church of St Henry.

Chapter 16

Married Life

On the day after their marriage, Weber and Caroline set off on their honeymoon. This took the form of a concert tour because Weber's funds were low, and he could reclaim some of the expenses from the Dresden Theatre. The couple worked their way back from Prague to Dresden via Heidelberg, Mannheim and a host of other places, including Giessen, where they performed some of Weber's liveliest comic songs. After passing through Weimar and Leipzig, where Weber proudly presented his bride to some of his former patrons, they arrived back at Dresden on 20 December, just in time to celebrate Christmas in their new home.

This early period of his marriage brought Weber much happiness. After waiting so long, and after facing so many distractions in the fraught working environment of Dresden, now, at last, he seemed to have found someone who could help shield him emotionally from the more abrasive side of life. He writes:

No man can appreciate more deeply the worth of the happiness heaven has bestowed on him. A bright, joyous temper now heals all the wounds of a long-tortured spirit. This sympathy with my joys and sorrows is a prize with which nothing can compare.

Weber had succeeded in persuading Caroline to give up her stage career by making it a condition of their marriage, and she seems to have settled happily into her new rôle as *Hausfrau*. Under these circumstances and with this support, 1817 ended well for Weber. Late into the night of New Year's Eve, he felt able to write in his diary:

The great important year has closed. May God still grant me the blessing, which He has hitherto so graciously accorded me; that I may have the power to make the dear one happy, and, as a brave artist, bring honour and advantage to my Fatherland! Amen!

Weber began the New Year with his hopes high, but before long his mood changed for the worse. This time, the problems facing him concerned the position of the orchestra in the theatre pit. One of the things that had upset Weber for some time, was that many of the brass instruments were positioned in such a way as to make it impossible for them either to be heard, or to see the conductor. In those days, the conductor did not stand at the front of the orchestra, but sat on a stool in front of the piano, in the middle of the orchestra, unable to see what was happening on stage.

Weber saw operatic production as a unity of music and drama, or rather as a drama articulated through music. He wanted full control over orchestra and stage, so, after pondering the problem for eight months, he began to experiment. During one of his own cantatas – a piece carefully chosen so as to minimise any offence that the changes might cause – Weber changed the position of the instruments. No-one seemed to notice. But later, when Weber used his newly-structured orchestra in Spontini's *La Vestale*, the King was struck by the altered appearance of the orchestra, and by the fact that the horns, which previously the walls of his box had muffled, now appeared to him to be very loud.

Count Vitzthum was summoned to receive the expression of royal disapproval, and he attempted to smoothe the matter over. But Weber's old enemy, Therese aus dem Winkel, saw her chance, and wrote an article condemning the new arrangements. Weber was, unfortunately, quick to retaliate. He wrote an article in reply, and included certain disparaging remarks about Italians. This was just what the opposition needed: Count Einsiedel expressed his indignation loudly and Weber was forced to put the orchestra back into its former position. Weber was mortified, and wrote a long letter to the King explaining his reasons and defending himself. But it was only through the hands of Count Einsiedel that letters could reach the royal cabinet, and, needless-to-say, the good Count made sure that Weber's petitions never got anywhere near the King. However, despite royal disapproval, and despite the hostile efforts of Therese aus dem Winkel, Weber did have some support. Public opinion was with him and, in the end, Einsiedel had to give way and to permit Weber's orchestral innovations.

Weber's life at Dresden was full of irritations of this kind; page after page of Max Maria's biography is devoted to them. But even though they took toll on his energies, Weber's artistic creativity was not crushed. Once he had locked himself into his study, Weber could shut out the outside world and its cares, and could concentrate on composing. In this way a considerable amount of music poured from his pen, though often it was hardly appreciated by the court. His Mass in E flat, for instance, was

106

commissioned by the King and first heard on 8 March 1818. As things turned out, the court absented itself from the church on that occasion, much to Weber's disappointment. But the general public didn't, and their approval eventually found its way to Prince Anton, who arranged for another performance to be organised. This time, the court did attend and Weber was ceremoniously presented with a ring as a sign of royal approval. Weber tried his hand at literary works as well as musical ones, and began writing comic novellas and parts of a novel. But the thing that made all this possible, in spite of the difficulties of the Dresden court, was Weber's love for Caroline. Afterwards, he was wont to say:

Caroline von Weber (née Brandt), in a drawing by her son Alexander.

They might have achieved their aim of getting rid of me for ever, because, between sorrow and hard labour, I was nigh bodily crushed down, had they chosen a less happy period of my life. The poison could not work, as love's balsam was ever ready with an antidote.

Caroline did her best to learn to cook, and she had occasional bouts of jealousy when she imagined that Weber's eye was roving. But, in general, the couple's life was happy and well-organised: they would rise early, and work until 10.00am, when Weber would go off to the theatre for rehearsals. They entertained a lot and, after his evenings at the theatre, Weber would seek the society of his male friends. They would meet in groups in various shops and houses, discussing poetry, scientific matters and politics. At other times they would go out together, Weber accompanying at the piano or guitar while Caroline sang. As spring came on, they found a house in the country, near the royal palace of Pillnitz, where Weber would work during the summer. It was in this little house that Weber was happiest, and in which he wrote some of his greatest music. Weber loved the beautiful countryside around Dresden – that part of Germany was known as 'Saxon Switzerland' because of its dramatic scenery, its chaotic masses of rock and its yawning ravines. It seems to have been this

The royal palace of Pillnitz.

108

scenery, and the setting of his house in it, that kept Weber in Dresden, despite tempting offers from elsewhere and the often tiresome conditions of work. He and Caroline were also tied to the place by their animals, whose numbers increased daily to include a large hound, a raven, a starling, a cat and an ape.

Weber had never had a strong constitution, and, despite his domestic happiness, he began to show symptoms of tuberculosis. He ignored them and kept on working, producing a steady stream of songs, incidental music and all the occasional pieces expected of a court composer. One of the more ambitious of these occasional pieces was the *Jubel-Kantata*, written to celebrate the 50th anniversary of the King's accession. Working on this cantata exhausted Weber, and in the autumn he and Caroline returned to Dresden somewhat depressed by the prospect of spending winter in the city. On their arrival, they were greeted by the bitter news that Weber's cantata would not after all be required; music by the Italian composer was to be substituted instead. Weber was humiliated, but once again public opinion came to his aid, and, at the express wish of the choir, his cantata did in fact receive a performance for the benefit of the destitute peasantry in the Hartz mountains.

Soon afterwards, Weber was cheered by the news that he would shortly be a father. To strengthen himself for the rôle, he went off to see two doctors. One was the royal physician, a man of the old school, complete with pigtail, gold shoe-buckles and gold snuffbox, but who applied the most violent remedies. The other was a smart, elegant young man, with black curly hair, a fine fiery eye and a soft, beautiful hand – a real lady-killer. Weber believed in both of these men, even though one recommended treatment to the stomach, the other to the throat.

Needless-to-say, the effects of the treatments were disastrous, and caused Weber to become nervous, irritable and morbidly suspicious. He began to behave somewhat erratically, showering Einsiedel with letters of complaint and taking almost any remark by the Italians as an insult. And indeed, he had his reasons. For almost two years, he had refrained from putting on a production of his own in Dresden, but in November 1818 he resolved to put *Silvana* before the Dresden public. As soon as the plan got out, the Italians did everything they could to frustrate it: singers went sick, those who didn't went to Morlacchi's rehearsals and not Weber's. In the end, Weber managed only three rehearsals of *Silvana* before he abandoned the project.

On 22 December, Caroline gave birth to her first child – a baby girl. The birth was difficult, and Weber was anxious for her. But his anxiety turned once again to mortification when, instead of the expected high-ranking officials, the royal family sent two servants as their representatives to the Baptism. Weber knew this was not a slight by the royal family itself – it was Einsiedel's doing – but he was deeply humiliated nevertheless.

The celebrations for the royal couple's 50th wedding anniversary were drawing near, and Weber hoped to impress the court with his Mass in G, composed specifically for the occasion. But, once again, the opposition stepped in to thwart his wishes. A few days before the performance, he was told that sections of his mass were to be replaced with parts by Morlacchi and Polledro, and it was only after the old, art-loving Prince Anton had intervened, that Weber could be soothed out of his fury. Prince Anton was himself an amateur composer, and he delighted in showing Weber his works and in having them corrected by him. In the end, the mass was indeed performed with insertions by the Italian composers, but Weber's attention was soon diverted by an unexpected commission that brought him great joy.

Prince Friedrich August was soon to be married to the Archduchess Caroline of Austria; Weber was asked to compose an opera to celebrate their union. The choice of subject was to be his. Once again, Kind undertook to be librettist, and, in ten days, he produced a version of *Alcindor*, one of the stories in *Arabian Nights*. All the magic of oriental romance began to fire Weber's imagination; he consulted endlessly about designs, stage-machines and suitable singers. In the midst of all this excitement he began to compose, but, in his failing state of health, such over-exertion proved dangerous, and for a month he was confined to his bed with a fever.

Caroline nursed him as best she could, but she too began to get ill, and so did her baby. At the end of March 1819 the child died, and the couple were devastated. Caroline was the first to rally, but Weber went into a depression which not even country air could alleviate. His doctor recommended a starvation diet, so Weber added acute pangs of hunger to his other torments. He became obsessed with food, and his meal-times began to be more of interest to him than his music. Gradually, as his health improved, he began to compose again. But then came the news that *Alcindor* was not, after all, wanted for the marriage celebrations. An allegorical cantata by Morlacchi was to be substituted instead.

Weber was shattered, but worse was yet to come. Count Vitzthum, his main support in government circles, resigned. 'Weber,' said Vitzthum, with tears of deep emotion in his eyes, 'we have both done our best for the good cause, and fought the good fight with zeal and energy; but I can do no more. I have sent in my resignation as Director of the Theatre. It has at last been accepted, and we must part.' As the two shook hands in farewell, it seemed that the future of German opera indeed looked bleak.

Julius Benedict in his later years.

However, the store of melodies that Weber had worked out for *Alcindor* but not yet written down, began to pour out of him. One of his most famous works – the *Invitation to the Waltz* – was written at this time, so was the Rondo in E flat.

Weber was further cheered by the fact that certain people took the trouble to visit him in Dresden. One was Heinrich Marschner, who, although only in his early 20s, had already written some impressive operas which Weber hoped to stage in Dresden. On another occasion, Weber was visited by the Berlin banker Mendelssohn-Bartholdy – Felix Mendelssohn's father – but it is not clear whether or not he was accompanied by his young son (only ten years old at the time). Then there was a meeting with Spohr.

Weber's hopes for German opera rose again in July 1819, when Count Brühl wrote to him from Berlin, saying that he hoped to put on *Der Freischütz* as the opening production in the new theatre there. So, once again, Weber got down to work on the score, and kept up his enthusiasm despite the later news that a work by Goethe would be used instead to open the theatre. Weber worked very fluently – there are hardly any corrections or second thoughts in the score – and before long he sent the work to Brühl.

Benedict describes 1820 as 'the culminating point' of Weber's musical career. But it started off a bit shakily: there were rows with the Italians over operas by Meyerbeer, and Caroline's second child died. But Weber was drawn out of himself by visits from, amongst others, the younger son of Mozart. He felt rather sorry for the young man, who seemed to be crushed by the burden of living up to his father's name.

Also at this time, Brühl came up with another commission, on this occasion for incidental music to Pius Alexander Wolff's play *Preciosa*, adapted from the novel by Cervantes called *The Little Gipsy*. Weber had always loved the exotic, and the songs he had heard sung by the Spanish soldiers in 1812 floated again in his mind. Plays, in those days, were accompanied by a great deal of orchestral music, and Weber described *Preciosa* as 'a heavy piece of work and an important one, more than half an opera'. Such was his enthusiasm for the project that it took him only seven weeks to complete it.

After such success with *Der Freischütz* and *Preciosa*, Weber's creative imagination was in full flight, and he turned his attention to *Die drei Pintos*, a libretto by his friend Theodor Hell. According to Max Maria, Weber created most of his music in his mind before committing it to paper. And although he fully intended to complete *Die drei Pintos*, he was destined never to do so. In fact, only seven pieces from it survive today, and they were used as the basis of completions by Meyerbeer and Mahler, amongst others.

111

As the summer of 1820 approached, Weber took a lease on a new country house on the banks of the Elbe, only 30 minutes' walk from the theatre. Caroline was rather unnerved by the thought of the path leading to the house: it was surrounded by gnarled trees and had been the scene of a murder only a few months before. To set her mind at rest, Weber took to carrying a pair of pistols and a sword stick, and he began to practise pistol shooting on a regular basis.

In May 1820, Spontini took over management of the Royal Theatre in Berlin. His idea of opera was colossal, costly and spectacular, and he was hardly the kind of man to think highly of what Weber was doing.

Weber decided to use his summer vacation to give a concert tour with Caroline. Their first engagement took place in Halle, where the concert hall was crammed with students and university performers all anxious to hear the composer of *Leyer und Schwert*. 'Would that I could hear my own songs sung from the very hearts of these brave German youths!' cried Weber to some friends. His wish was gratified. The university of Halle had a strong musical tradition, and there were several singing clubs among the students. At about 10.00 in the evening, more than 400 students gathered in front of Weber's house. After a *vivat*, which seemed to go on for ever, several of Weber's songs were sung in full chorus by the assembled multitude.

The Webers left Halle in the highest spirits, loaded with presents and copies of books by admiring academics. A few days later they arrived in Göttingen – another university town. Once again, the students gave Weber a rapturous welcome, and crowded outside his hotel room to sing his *Song of Freedom*.

The contrast between this and his life at Dresden did not escape Weber. He wrote: 'If I am everywhere to be warmed by such fire as this, I can console myself for the cold chill thrown on me in Dresden.'

But before long, all this excitement proved too much – both Weber and Caroline became ill and had to abandon any idea of a concert in Hanover. On the way to Bremen their carriage overturned; their concert in the city was a success, but in Hamburg Caroline discovered she was pregnant and had to take to her bed once again. Weber continued the tour by himself, driving first to Eutin, his birthplace, where he received a hero's welcome.

Then he made his way to the port at Kiel, where he had to wait for a few days until a storm abated and the steamer could take him to Copenhagen. His concerts in Kiel were not successful, but any despondency he might have felt was quickly dispelled by the majesty of the marine scenery. True to form, he described his experiences in a letter to Caroline:

I left land by splendid moonlight and a bright starry heaven. The receding shore, with its glaring lighthouse, had a magical effect . . . The waves were rough, however, and the wind blew hard; and the poor landsman had to pay his tribute to Neptune. But how great were the glories of the rising sun! They repaid for all . . . How many a blessing did I waft to my own dear one on that great greeting of the morning!

Weber's reception in Copenhagen exceeded his wildest dreams. He was received both by the intellectuals of the town and by royalty; he was sent a gold snuffbox by the Count; and, to top it all, he made an enormous profit from his concerts.

However, despite all his success, Weber's thoughts were with Caroline. So, as soon as his concerts in Copenhagen were over, he hastened back to Hamburg. He was pleased to find his wife in much better health, and able to face the return journey to Dresden. It was here, in Hamburg, that the Webers picked up their pet monkey 'Schnuff', who, on the way back caused some anxiety, as Max Maria recounts:

Caroline's condition rendered short day-journeys necessary; and by this arrangement they were obliged to sleep one night in a small Hanoverian town. The room in which they were lodged was spectral in its aspect; the fire snorted on the wide hearth; the windows rattled in the gusty wind. They crept to bed, chilled with the ghostly and lugubrious aspect of the apartment. Presently, they were waked from their first slumber by a rustling sound, then a strange knocking. Weber sprang from the bed, seized his pistols, and flung open the door. Nothing was to be heard in the dark passage but the howling of the wind. Again those strange unearthly sounds. A light was struck. A search was made round the room, while Caroline lay shivering with fear. Nothing was to be seen; but still those sounds. At last the mystery was solved. Master Schnuff, who had been forgotten, lay on his back in his travelling-chest, tormented by a simian nightmare. After a hearty laugh, the wearied couple were able to rest again from their spectral terrors.

They arrived back in Dresden in early November, just in time to celebrate their joint fête-day with a masquerade. Their large dog was transformed into an elephant, their cat into a donkey with panniers, whilst their monkey marched proudly behind in petticoat, hat, feathers and muff.

During his tour, Weber had been given ample proof of the esteem in which he was held in other German cities, but even in Dresden a few incidents served to increase his standing in the eyes of the public. One of these was his conducting of *The Magic Flute* from memory, at a time when such a thing was unknown. Then the overture to *Der Freischütz* was given its first performance. However, one of the things that gave most pleasure to Weber was

Weber, a drawing of the composer after tuberculosis began to take its toll on his health.

the arrival in Dresden of Julius Benedict, 15-year-old son of a wealthy banker, who came armed with strong recommendations from Hummel to ask Weber for lessons. Benedict later wrote:

I shall never forget the impression of my first meeting with him. Ascending the winding staircase, which led to his modest home on the third storey of a house in the old market-place, I found him sitting at his desk, and occupied with the pianoforte arrangement of his *Freischütz*. The dire disease, which all too soon was to carry him off, had made its mark on his noble features; the projecting cheekbones, the general emaciation, told their sad tale. But in his clear blue eyes, too often concealed by spectacles, in his mighty forehead, fringed by a few straggling locks, in the sweet expression of his mouth, in the very tone of

114

his weak but melodious voice, there was a magic power which attracted irresistibly all who approached him. He received me with the utmost kindness, and, though overwhelmed with double duties during the temporary absence of Morlacchi, he found time to give me daily lessons for a considerable period.

On 15 March 1820, *Preciosa* was given its first performance in Berlin. Weber's music went down well with the public, auguring well for the more important première of *Der Freischütz* which was due to follow soon after.

Chapter 17

Der Freischütz

The opening of the new Berlin Theatre was scheduled for the end of March; *Der Freischütz* was to be the first operatic production, opening in May. Weber left the casting to Brühl, as he didn't know enough about singers in Berlin to cast the opera himself. On 4 May, he arrived in the Prussian capital and went, as usual, to stay with the Beers.

But in Berlin, as in Dresden, operatic life was divided into opposing factions. Like Dresden, the court favoured Italian opera, in this case that grand, heroic type characteristic of Spontini. Spontini's arrogant personality and his evident contempt for German culture quickly made him very unpopular with the Berlin public. However, Spontini was a superb politician, and his position in Berlin seemed unassailable. He was about to produce his spectacular opera *Olympia*; and, with immense sums of money being lavished on it, many of Weber's friends feared that *Der Freischütz* would come off badly in comparison. Art, in those days, was a highly emotive affair; passions ran high and sides were taken. As Max Maria says:

It was always the destiny of Weber, who arrived at a time of transition in the history of art in Germany, to see his works produced under the influence of excited party-spirit. He himself felt that his new venture must either raise him to a high pinnacle, and render an enormous service to the cause of German art, or be carried to the grave with scorn and mockery. There was no middle course. It was to be a battle for life or death.

When he arrived in Berlin, Weber found that preparations for his opera had already begun. However, on inspecting the proposed scenery, he found it too classical – insufficiently imaginative and fantastical. He told the designer:

Your ideas are altogether too delicate for such a subject as *Freischütz* . . . They would be more fitting for *Hamlet* or *Macbeth*. What has my music

116

The composer Gasparo Spontini.

to do with misty forms and grinning rocks? Give me my owl with flaming eyes, real fluttering bats; spare neither spectres or skeletons; and let the horrors go *crescendo* by every ball . . . Do away with all your embroidery, and buttons, and green tights, and dancing-shoes, and gold lace, and give me the rough wild unadorned costume of the Thirty-Years War.

Weber carefully took his singers through their rôles and, on 21 May, rehearsals began at the theatre. Things went well – any doubts and bewilderments caused by the novelty and unfamiliarity of such original music were quickly dispelled, and all went smoothly until the day of the dress rehearsal. Benedict describes the scene:

117

Stage design by Carl Gropius for the first performance of *Der Freischütz*.

The composer was received with acclamation by all the principals, chorus and orchestra, who looked forward with the utmost confidence to the next day; but the accessories, machinery, etc., were still woefully deficient, principally in one of the most important scenes – the Wolf's Glen. The celebrated painter, Gropius, had furnished splendid decorations for the limited stage of the Berlin Theatre. The main object in the construction of the new house, however, had been to establish a permanent home for German drama, and for light operas such as Boïeldieu's *Jean de Paris*, *le Petit Chaperon rouge*, etc. Therefore, scanty accommodation was given to the machinists for sensational effects. Thus the gigantic owl, intended to flap its wings, and whose glowing eyes were supplied by two little oil lamps, met with an accident disabling one of the wings, whilst the threatening eyes of the night-bird resembled small street lanterns. The fiery carriage was so badly contrived that the fireworks never went off at all, and a common empty wheel, garnished with inoffensive crackers and rockets, ludicrously crossed the stage. The wild hunt, painted on canvas, could not be distinctly seen from the front; Caspar, in his eagerness, had given the cue, 'Seven! the wild hunt: Zamiel, help!' too soon, thus destroying the effect of the infernal chorus, and upsetting all the arrangements of the stage manager.

Weber was not in the mood to be downcast by this: instead, he went home to spend two tranquil hours finishing the *Concertstück* in F minor. And indeed, when he took his place on the conductor's

118

a)

b)

c)

d)

e)

Costume designs for *Der Freischütz*:
a) Agathe
b) and c) Agathe in her wedding dress
d) Zamiel and Caspar
e) Max

podium and was greeted with rapturous applause, he had good reason to imagine that his hour had come. The performance went without a hitch, and the opera was a great success. To Max Maria, critics, artists and dilettanti all appeared intoxicated, and they entertained Weber to a supper attended by many of the most eminent literary men in Berlin.

However, in the papers next morning, the enthusiasm of the critics was decidedly lukewarm. According to Max Maria, the critics liked the sound of the music, but 'they could never quite forgive its audacious novelty', and they complained that:

. . . classical repose was sacrificed to effect, that the originality was often monstrous, that the characterisation bordered on caricature, that

Königliche Schauspiele.

Montag, den 18. Juny 1821.

Im Schauspielhause.
Zum Erstenmale:

Der Freischütz.

Oper in 3 Abtheilungen (zum Theil nach dem Volksmährchen: Der Freischütz),
von F. Kind. Musik von Carl Maria v. Weber.

Personen:

Ottokar, regierender Graf	Hr. Rebenstein.
Cuno, gräflicher Erbförster	Hr. Wauer.
Agathe, seine Tochter	Mad. Seidler.
Aennchen, eine junge Verwandte	Mlle. Joh. Eunike.
Caspar, erster } Jägerbursch	Hr. Blume.
Max, zweiter	Hr. Stümer.
Samiel, der schwarze Jäger	Hr. Hillebrand.
Ein Eremit	Hr. Gern.
Kilian, ein reicher Bauer	Hr. Wiedemann.
Brautjungfern	Mlle. Henr. Reinwald rc.
Jäger und Gefolge des Grafen Hr. Michaelis. Hr. Titschow. Hr. Buggenhagen rc.	
Landleute und Musikanten.	
Erscheinungen.	

Scene: In Böhmen.   Zeit: kurz nach Beendigung des dreißigjährigen Krieges.
Die sämmtlich neuen Decorationen sind von dem Königl. Decorations-Maler Herrn Gropius
gezeichnet und gemalt.

Arienbücher sind das Stück für 4 Groschen an der Kasse zu haben.

Zu dieser Vorstellung sind nur noch Parterre-Billets à 12 Gr. und Amphitheater-Billets à 6 Gr. zu haben.

Anzeige.

Im Opernhause: Der Jude, Schauspiel in 5 Abtheilungen, nach dem Englischen des Cumberland. Hierauf: Der Nachtwächter, Posse in 1 Aufzug, von Th. Körner.

Dienstag den 19. Juny. Im Opernhause: Die Jungfrau von Orleans, romantische Tragödie in 5 Abtheilungen, von Schiller.

Bekanntmachung.

In der Buchhandlung von Duncker und Humblot, französische Straße Nr. 20 a. wird verkauft:
E. v. Houwald das Bild, Trauerspiel in 5 Akten, 1 Rthlr. 12 Gr.
Dessen der Leuchtthurm; die Heimkehr; zwei Trauerspiele, 1 Rthlr.
Bäuerle komisches Theater, 3tet Band, (enthält: die Gespensterfamilie; der Fiacker als Marquis; der verwünschte Prinz), 1 Rthlr. 8 Gr.
Müllners Spiele für die Bühne, Band 1 und 2, (enthalten: der neun und zwanzigste Februar; die Vertrauten; der angolische Kater; die Zurückkunft aus Surinam; die Zweiflerin; die großen Kinder; der Wahn; der Blitz; die Onkelei), 3 Rthlr. 8 Gr.

Anfang 6 Uhr; Ende 9 Uhr.

Die Kasse wird um 5 Uhr geöffnet.

Billing for *Der Freischütz.*

120

musical impossibilities were 'music no more'. Many ceaselessly repeated that the opera owed the greater part of its success to the devilry and fireworks. This last assertion struck Weber so forcibly, that, in a subsequent letter to Lichtenstein, he wrote: 'Had not I the testimony of so many good and honourable judges, I myself might have been led to think that I owed all my success to Monsieur Zamiel.'

But, whatever the critics may have thought, public opinion was firmly behind Weber. Both inside the theatre and outside, audience enthusiasm was tremendous. In the light of this, it is surprising that a concert that Weber put on in the theatre did not make much of a profit, even though it contained the newly finished *Concertstück*. Weber shared the concert with the French violinist Alexandre Boucher, who played some variations on a Norwegian melody that Weber had written for him. But the Frenchman's excitement got the better of him, and at one point in the piece:

. . . he suddenly stopped playing, went through a host of *tremolandos*, *pizzicatos*, and other tricks on his instrument, imitated the trumpet-tones announcing the entrance of Zamiel, and plunged into a wild *olla podrida* on melodies from *Der Freischütz*, in which he finally bewildered and lost himself entirely. Then, throwing down his violin, he sprang upon Weber, and embraced the struggling composer before all the spectators with the words, almost choked by well-acted emotion, '*Ah! grand maître! que je t'aime! que je t'admire!*'

Needless-to-say, the public loved every minute of this extra-ordinary display, and took the opportunity to assert their admiration for Weber all the more strongly.

On 1 July 1821, after an absence of two wonderful months, the Webers arrived back in Dresden. Even though the whole of Europe was ringing with his name, the Dresdeners treated him with complete indifference. 'It was the same old story', laments Max Maria. 'What is a prophet in his own country?'

Caroline's health was now giving cause for alarm, so Weber arranged that she should take the waters at Spandau. After installing her there, he started back, hoping to return to Dresden before nightfall. But just as the ferry pulled out to carry him over the river Elbe, a storm broke, and the horses attached to his carriage panicked. They almost dragged the carriage over the side of the boat, but the boatmen eventually managed to calm them down. Weber was so unnerved by this flirtation with death that he drew up his will that night before going to bed.

Meanwhile, Friedrich Kind was behaving less than graciously over the success of *Der Freischütz*. Weber offered him some of the box-office takings (although he was under no contractual obligation to do so) because they had been very considerable, and he wished to pay tribute to the part Kind had played in the success. Unfortunately, Kind was not to be humoured, and was jealous of the praise heaped upon the composer. Complaining that every creature in the theatre, even the lamp-man, was considered more important than the poet, he turned down the gift and asked to be left alone. Weber tried hard to appease his old friend, but all in vain, and the one successful relationship that he had ever had with a librettist came to a sticky end.

But something altogether more positive happened next. Wilhelm II, Elector of Hesse-Cassel, decided to reform his theatre, and took steps to hire the best *Kapellmeister* in Germany for the purpose. His agent, Feige, was instructed to look for such a man, and he wrote at once to Weber, offering him an annual salary of 2500 thalers, a pension and the appointment for life. Weber wrote to Caroline:

It's a thousand thalers more than I have here, but the more I reflect upon leaving Dresden, the heavier falls the weight upon my heart. I handed over Feige's letter to Herr von Könneritz [Count Vitzthum's successor]. He read it without a word. I dined with him yesterday, and drove over to Pillnitz with him: but he still held his peace; and I was too shy to speak on the matter myself. I cannot thrust such an offer aside as though it were nothing . . . but in truth you cannot be more attached to Dresden than I am.

As time went by and as Weber still did not hear anything, he wrote to Könneritz, pointing out that, although he was honoured to have a position in Dresden, he nevertheless had a duty to his family, and couldn't overlook the fact that his talents appeared under-esteemed in Dresden when compared with the rest of Germany. In the end he stayed on in Dresden with an increased salary, while the position at Cassel was filled by Spohr, on Weber's recommendation.

Meanwhile, *Der Freischütz* was being performed all over Europe. It was given at Breslau, Prague, Carlsruhe, Pest, Copenhagen, Königsberg and Hanover, always with great success. In Vienna certain changes were made under orders from the censor. The Emperor had forbidden firearms to be used on stage, so the guns in *Freischütz* had to be exchanged for crossbows, and, as hermits were not permitted either, the rôle of Zamiel was cut. Weber was outraged by the way his work was hacked about, but at least in Vienna it was actually staged.

Back home in Dresden, every intrigue was tried, every pretext invented and every difficulty created by the Italians, to prevent a production. After considerable effort, Weber secured permission from the King to stage it early in 1822, but all the hostile words of the opposition stayed in people's minds, and preparations went ahead without much enthusiasm on the part of the performers. As Max Maria said, 'the enemies of German opera rubbed their hands triumphantly.'

Chapter 18

Euryanthe

Despite the cuts that the censor had insisted on, *Der Freischütz* went down very well in Vienna, and soon afterwards Weber was invited by Domenico Barbaja, one of the leading Viennese impresarios of the time, to write a new opera for the 1822–23 season. Weber was overjoyed by the commission and he wrote back immediately, inquiring as to exact conditions, not only for himself but for the author of the libretto too. The answer from Barbaja contained an invitation for Weber to come – all expenses paid – to the city to study the singers, chorus and theatre for himself.

Weber began to search for a book in earnest, and here, unfortunately, things went rather less well. He thought of the *Cid*, which Kind had at one time begun to write, but the poet was still jealous and refused to collaborate. He was offered a libretto on Dido, but turned it down as the story had been used so often before. Then he heard a reading given by Helmine von Chezy, and it struck him that she might be able to provide him with what he sought. Helmine herself was delighted by the invitation, and a few days later she proposed a whole list of subjects, chiefly borrowed from *Romantic Poems of the Middle Ages* by her friend Friedrich Schlegel. Weber chose one based on an old French romance entitled *Histoire de Gérard de Nevers et de la belle et vertueuse Euryanthe, sa Mie*.

Weber must have known that this story was entirely undramatic, and it is hard to understand how he came to choose it. Perhaps he was led astray by all the episodical incidents of fire-spitting dragons, giants, tournaments, magic rings and murders, that it contained. It isn't impossible to use material such as this for an operatic libretto, as Wagner was later to prove, but, unfortunately, Helmine was not the poet Wagner was, nor did she have his understanding of dramatic form.

She was a remarkable lady with a rather dubious background, a rather difficult temper, and a reputation as a bluestocking. As things turned out, Helmine was not the ideal collaborator for Weber. He returned her first draft requesting almost total revision, and it was only after about six months that the script began to look as if it could be workable.

Weber was still hoping to finish *Die drei Pintos* and to dedicate it to the King. Preferring to do this before embarking on the new opera for Vienna, he wrote to Count Einsiedel in the hope that the King would express his approval and arrangements could begin for the production. What happened instead distressed Weber to the point of breaking his health. Einsiedel wrote back saying that, as Weber had already been given permission to have *Der Freischütz* performed, he could hardly expect to put on another of his works so soon.

Despite this insult, Weber went on with preparations for *Freischütz* in Dresden, taking all the more care, as he knew that any failure or error, however small, would be seized upon and gloated over by the Italian faction. He superintended all the backstage and scenic efforts as well as the music and, in doing so, incurred the disapproval of his friend Tieck. Tieck was wont to say that it did not become a man of genius and influence to display so much small-minded anxiety about scenery, decoration and 'machinery nonsense'; but Weber clung to his principle that the dramatic stage should combine, as much as possible, all the excellencies of each sister art, and the two men frequently quarrelled.

When the performance eventually took place, it was a magnificent success; Weber was cheered and acclaimed as he had never been before in Dresden. It was a triumphant night, but, even so, the press comment next day was not so euphoric. The Vienna press in particular was unimpressed – and this worried Weber as it did not augur well for *Euryanthe*.

On 10 February, Weber left for Vienna. Before he departed, he handed Caroline a sealed letter, to be opened only in case of his death. It contained his will, and a letter declaring his unwavering love for her.

Three days later, he arrived in Prague where he heard Henriette Sontag, then only 18. Although Weber was not very impressed by her then, she was later to become his Euryanthe. After three further days of travelling, he arrived in Vienna and heard a performance of *Der Freischütz*, mutilated on the censor's orders. Shocked as he was by this, Weber soon began to enjoy himself and feel he was wanted. He met Schubert, tried to patch up a quarrel with Salieri, and frequented aristocratic and intellectual circles. But the pace proved too much for him and he fell ill, returning to Dresden as soon as he was able.

On 25 April, Caroline gave birth to a son, christened two days

Antonio Salieri, the Italian composer.

later as Max Maria. After several unsuccessful pregnancies, the Webers at last found themselves with a baby that was going to survive. Cheered by this new arrival, Weber began work on *Euryanthe*. But his spirit was being worn down – visits from unwelcome guests, a road accident when once again his carriage upturned, and an unsuccessful run of *Preciosa* all continued to take their toll on him. It was while he was in this state of mind that he finished his Fourth Piano Sonata. Julius Benedict gives an indication of the kind of work it is:

The first movement, according to Weber, portrays in mournful strains the state of a sufferer from fixed melancholy and despondency, with occasional glimpses of hope, which are, however, always darkened and crushed. The second movement describes an outburst of rage and insanity; the Andante in C is of a consolatory nature, and fitly expresses the partly successful entreaties of friendship and affection endeavouring to calm the patient, though there is an undercurrent of agitation of evil augury. The last movement, a wild fantastic Tarantella, with only a few snatches of melody, finishes in exhaustion and death.

Weber could transfer his attention from one piece to another with amazing rapidity – as soon as he had finished the sonata he wrote a little *Marcia Vivace* for the ten trumpets of the Prussian Black Hussars, which he later included in *Euryanthe*.

But the more he got involved with *Euryanthe*, the more Weber realised that Chezy was going to prove an unreliable librettist. He considered the material she was sending him to be dreadful, and began to hold preliminary discussions with other writers.

Unfortunately, one of the most interesting parts of Weber's correspondence is lost. He wrote to Beethoven discussing plans for a Dresden production of *Fidelio*, but only Weber's first letter and none of Beethoven's replies survive.

The first page of the manuscript for *Euryanthe*.

On one occasion, Weber had to put on a performance of *Preciosa* at short notice, when Ludwig I of Bavaria visited Dresden: the King lost interest in a work by Rossini, and demanded 'give me something by your young wizard Weber!'

Greatly cheered by this public expression of esteem, Weber, on 8 May, finally made it out to his summer residence, where he worked on *Euryanthe* as much as he could. Often, he would work for six or eight hours without a break, and the work was finished by the end of August, except for the overture, which Weber wrote in the first week of September.

In the middle of September, Weber left for Vienna, with Julius Benedict as his assistant, and carrying the score of *Euryanthe* with him. No sooner had he arrived in the Austrian capital, than he was seized by anxiety. Once more, he felt that his 'evil star' was shedding its blighting influence over him, and Max Maria tells us 'no reasoning could efface from his mind this depressing conviction.' Certainly there were grounds for worry: Vienna was in the throes of a Rossini-craze and if the Viennese weren't listening to Rossini, then they might just as likely be listening to some imitation of *Freischütz*. It's not common to find composers regretting the success of their works, but on this occasion Weber was worried lest the new work pale into insignificance when compared with the old!

However there was, in fact, a great deal of support for Weber in Vienna. As Max Maria reports:

A great portion of the intelligence, taste, cultivation, and true artistic feeling was already on his side. In the musical emporium of Steiner-Haslinger, where the influential music critics of the time were wont to stroll in to look at the newest scores, chat upon the musical topics of the day, and give their opinion with unscrupulous swagger, Weber found also more confederates than he had expected. He was aware that he could rely upon the lower classes, who hated the Italian opera, and looked askance and sulkily on its supporters among the court, the noble officials, and the garrison; but he was unwilling to take any direct steps to court their favour. Circumstances led him in a direction, which he followed almost against his own will, but which was to lead him into the very midst of a camp, where he was to find confederate powers who ranged themselves wholly on his side.

One of the most frequent visitors to Steiner's music shop was Beethoven, and it was there that Benedict happened to overhear him talking about *Euryanthe*. Weber longed to visit the great composer, but had been put off by the many rumours regarding Beethoven's rude and uncouth manners to his visitors. But, by now, he was apparently mellowing. Max Maria takes up the story:

Weber knew, then, that he had earned Beethoven's respect before his visit. But he felt strangely moved when he entered the great man's poor desolate-looking room. All lay in the wildest disorder – music, money, clothing, on the floor – linen from the wash upon the dirty bed – broken

Ludwig van Beethoven's house.

coffee-cups upon the table. The open pianoforte was covered thickly with dust. Beethoven entered to greet his visitors. He recognised Weber without a word, embraced him energetically, shouting out, 'There you are, my boy; you are a devil of a fellow! God bless you!', handed him at once his famous tablets, then pushed a heap of music from the old sofa, threw himself upon it, and, during a flow of conversation, commenced dressing himself to go out.

Beethoven began with a string of complaints, then he dragged Weber off to the *Sauerhof*, where he regularly dined. Weber wrote afterwards:

Here we dined together in the happiest mood. The rough, repulsive man paid me as much attention as if I were a lady to whom he was making court, and served me at table with the most delicate care. How proud I felt to receive all this kindness and affectionate regard from the great master-spirit! The day will remain forever impressed on my mind, as well as on that of all who were present.

When the time came to depart, Beethoven embraced Weber as though he could not bear to part with him. When at last they tore themselves away, Beethoven roared, 'Success to your new opera!

Beethoven c. 1823.

129

If I can, I will come on your first night.' As things turned out, however, Beethoven didn't make it on that night, and the two men never met again.

Weber conducted rehearsals of *Euryanthe* in his usual thorough-going manner. He began by reading the story aloud, declaiming all the various parts with such urgency and passion that the stage manager said that he'd missed his vocation as an actor, and laughingly offered him an engagement on the spot! Weber knew that when an opera singer doesn't understand the plot – that is, when he doesn't understand the motivation for his actions and his words – then he is likely to go wrong, and the show will fall to pieces. But, as the readings went on, it became clear just how garbled the libretto was – 'Who are these dead lovers, Udo and Emma?' the singers asked. 'Why does Euryanthe set so much store by their secret?' 'Why doesn't the woman defend herself, and tell Lysiart he is a liar to his face?'

Despite these problems of comprehension of the plot, the singers loved working on the opera, and gave freely of their time to perfect their parts. Even the chorus asked for extra rehearsals, to the amazement of the management. Weber was delighted with the progress they made, but his life was not without its problems. Various rumours spread around Vienna to the effect that *Euryanthe* would most likely fail. Even Franz Schubert added fuel to the fire with such remarks as 'How Weber will manage I can't conceive. He would do better to leave it all alone.'

Then there was Helmine von Chezy, who began fussing over the libretto, making constant and ineffectual changes to the text, and plaguing Weber with demands for more money. Eventually, Weber agreed to split the proceeds with her fifty–fifty. Then she started demanding payment in advance, letting loose on Weber a barrage of abusive letters and bullying messages almost every hour of the day. Weber described himself as 'sick with disgust', but worse was to follow. Helmine rushed round Vienna, telling such stories of Weber's cruelty and avarice that tongues began to wag their disapproval. By hitting Weber in this way, Helmine won the battle and Weber was forced to pay her off by dipping into his own pocket.

Strangely enough, so great was the superstitious aspect of Weber's nature, that he was almost grateful for incidents such as these, believing that they might deflect the malignant attention of his 'evil star' away from *Euryanthe*. But things weren't to be so easy. When the opera was given its first complete run-through, it was found to last four hours, and its colossal length soon became the butt of jokes around Vienna. 'Weber writes for eternity, so of course his opera must be eternally long', went one, and Weber himself lamented that perhaps his *Euryanthe* should be called *Ennuyante*.

In spite of all these problems, the dress rehearsal went well. The theatre was full; the appearance of a new opera was an event of considerable social importance in Metternich's Vienna, and anybody of any social and artistic standing was there. They seemed to approve of the piece and hopes of a success were high as the theatre began to fill for the first night. Even now, however, Helmine von Chezy contrived to make an exhibition of herself. Just as the performance was due to start, she forced her way noisily through the stalls, shrieking 'Make room! Make room for me, I say! I tell you I am the poetess! The poetess!' – 'The poetess! The poetess!' yelled the laughing crowd, taking up the refrain.

In this boisterous atmosphere, Weber made his way to the conductor's rostrum, and the jeering laughter turned to applause. Eventually, Weber managed to get silence in the house, and *Euryanthe* began. Various numbers appealed particularly to the audience, and they were repeated – a good idea in principle – but it meant that the show dragged on long after its four hour duration. In addition, the intervals and pauses between scenes were lengthy, and both audience and cast began to get very tired indeed as the evening wore on.

To the dismay of Weber's friends, boxes and stalls gradually began to empty. Nevertheless, the première was considered a brilliant success, and Weber was well-satisfied when he wrote to his wife: 'All the company seemed in a state of ecstasy: singers, choruses, orchestra – all were drunk, as it were, with joy.'

Not everyone shared Weber's enthusiasm, though. Franz

Franz Schubert, 1825.

131

Schubert denounced Weber's opera as utterly unmusical, deficient in all form and order, without any solid foundation for the display of real talent, and – as far as technique and craft of composition were concerned – clear evidence that the composer had studied in the school of a mere mountebank. He continued:

The man abuses Rossini and yet, when he does contrive to catch a scrap of melody, he is sure to crush it to death, like a mouse in a trap, with his overwhelming orchestration.

Weber stayed in Vienna until the beginning of November, when he had an audience with the Emperor (who had accepted the dedication of *Euryanthe*).

Then he set out for Prague. The management of his old theatre there had planned a gala to celebrate the 50th performance of *Der Freischütz*; and they had postponed the performance in order that Weber might conduct it himself.

On returning to Dresden he discovered, much to his delight, that he could employ an assistant to help him with all the additional duties heaped upon his shoulders through the prolonged absence of Morlacchi. For a long time, Weber had hoped that his friend Gänsbacher would take up this post, and he wrote to give him the good news at once. But Gänsbacher, tired of waiting, had only a few days before accepted the post of *Kapellmeister* at St Stephen's cathedral in Vienna. Weber was stunned by the news, as he'd been looking forward to collaborating with one of his oldest and dearest friends, and his health took a turn for the worse.

After all his exertions on *Euryanthe*, Weber's creative powers were exhausted: between 19 October 1823 and 23 January 1825 he composed only one short song. *Euryanthe* itself was not doing particularly well. After Weber had left Vienna, the cast seemed to flag, cuts were made which ruined the opera's already precarious dramatic structure, and, by the 8th performance, the theatre was nearly empty. In some cities the opera had fallen flat, in others its reception was decidedly lukewarm. Weber was, naturally enough, disheartened, as is clear from this letter to Danzi:

The expectations of the masses have been puffed up to such an absurd and impossible pitch by the wonderful success of *Der Freischütz* that now, when I lay before them a simple, serious work, which only aims at truth of expression, passion and characteristic delineation, without any of the exciting elements of its predecessor, what can I expect? Be it as God wills!

But God's will is unpredictable, and consolation was on hand from an unexpected quarter. When, after only 11 rehearsals,

Euryanthe was staged at Dresden, it was a brilliant triumph. Weber at last felt that he was rising above the petty in-fighting and nationalistic factions, and he was all the more eager to have the work put on in Berlin. But to do this, he had to come up against Spontini again, and the Italian, jealous of his territory, did everything he could to frustrate Weber's ambitions. After an acrimonious exchange of correspondence, Weber withdrew his score, his nerves shattered. He now no longer had the strength to undertake the country walks which had been such a source of solace in earlier days and, in search of a rest, set out for Marienbad. He wrote to Caroline:

I have not the slightest yearning for piano or music-paper. I feel as if I must have been a tailor, and no composer, all my life . . . I never would have believed that I could ever feel this disgust for work. But oh! If it should always continue so! Shall I ever again find a single thought within me? Now there is nothing – nothing. I feel as if I have never composed a note in my life, and that the operas could never have been really mine.

Fortunately, other events intervened to rouse Weber from his apathy. One was an invitation from Paris, asking him for new operas and promising conducting engagements. But Weber hesitated – he couldn't rid himself of his aversion to work. Another came from Charles Kemble of the Covent Garden Theatre in London, once again requesting a new opera, and promising conducting engagements.

Weber's friends urged him to accept the English offer, and eventually he did so, out of respect both for England and for the illustrious family to which Charles Kemble belonged. But he worried about the decision for a long time. For some while now, Weber had been haunted by the idea that his days were numbered and that his end was near. Money had begun to preoccupy him – not out of greed for himself, but out of anxiety for his family. Weber was not a rich man; he had paid off his father's debts and his own, but he had very little to pass on to his wife and children. With this in mind, he asked his friend Dr Hedenus for a frank opinion about the state of his health. The doctor's verdict was clear:

If you give up all idea of composing or conducting and spend a year, at least, in Italy doing absolutely nothing, you may live for another five or six years. If you don't, it can only be a matter of weeks!

Weber replied:

Ah, well, I can never expect to secure a provision for my wife and family by dragging out my life, uselessly, for a few years longer. In England there is a chance of my getting some return for my labours, by which I may leave them at least some means which I could not otherwise procure. Be it as God wills!

In the middle of September, Kemble wrote back, offering Weber a completely free choice of subject for the new opera, but begging him at the same time to choose a typically German one – perhaps *Faust* or *Oberon*. Weber was taken by the idea of *Oberon*, and asked Kemble to send him a libretto as soon as possible. He also asked for details of the singers likely to be employed, any special areas of expertise they might have, and how they looked on stage. Kemble was detailed in his replies, even though the two men had a number of disagreements over Weber's fee.

The promised libretto did not arrive for some time, but meanwhile Weber set to work learning English, feeling that he should enter as fully as possible into the artistic spirit of the place where his new work would be performed. Between 2 October 1824 and 11 February 1826, he had 153 lessons, and, by the end of them, could speak proficiently and carry on a fluent correspondence in his new language.

Early in 1825, Weber received the libretto for *Oberon*, written by James Robinson Planché. On 27 February he began to write the music, but no sooner had he started than he was forced to break off again.

Things had changed in the management of the Dresden Theatre and Weber feared they would turn out to be to his disadvantage. The new Director General was Wolf von Lüttichau, a handsome, reckless and generally uncultured courtier, a fan of the Italian school of opera, and a disciple of Weber's enemy, Count Einsiedel. In addition, the Italian Opera at Dresden was flourishing as never before; it had excellent singers and was enjoying unprecedented success with the public. A staging of Spohr's German opera *Jessonda*, however, despite an excellent performance, had left the public cold and indifferent. These problems at home hit Weber hard, and he was further depressed when he heard that pirated performances of his works were being staged in Paris.

Castil-Blaze, a famous musicologist and critic, had adapted *Der Freischütz* by changing the setting to Scotland and commissioning a new libretto. He had staged his new version at the Odeon Theatre in Paris with great success, and had pocketed all the receipts for himself. Not only did Weber lose money that was rightfully his, but his chances of ever staging the genuine opera in Paris were much reduced by these events. Castil-Blaze, meanwhile, was cashing in as quickly as he could, and also staged a new version of *Preciosa*. Weber wrote letters of protest to the management of the theatre and to Castil-Blaze himself, but they all went unanswered. There was little Weber could do, and the experience was extremely galling for a man desperate to secure enough funds to provide for his wife and family – especially when, in January 1825, Caroline gave birth to another son, Alexander.

Meanwhile, Italian opera in Dresden continued to outdo the German in popular esteem. Morlacchi's *Tebaldo ed Isolina* had been rapturously received, whereas Weber's production of Cherubini's *Faniska* had flopped. With his spirits at a low ebb, Weber turned down an invitation from Count Brühl in Berlin to compose witches music for *Macbeth*. Instead, he set out at the beginning of April to take the waters at Ems, stopping off at various places on the way.

On the Prussian frontier (where the customs officers declined to examine his luggage out of respect for his compositions), he was told that Spontini had left Berlin for a while, making it possible to stage *Euryanthe* there. Fortified by this news, Weber arrived in Weimar where he stayed with his friend, the composer Hummel. While in Weimar, he met Goethe's son, who pressed him to pay

Goethe, 1823.

his father a visit. Weber was uneasy – he knew that Goethe had earlier expressed himself as no admirer of 'a talent of the mushroom order' – but he, at last, succumbed to the pressure. It was a mistake. Goethe kept him waiting for ages in his anteroom, even sending out twice to inquire 'what the man's name was'. When Weber was at last admitted to the great man's presence, he was received with indifference and dismissed very quickly and tersely. Weber was mortified and suffered a relapse. He took to his bed for two days, before moving on to Gotha and then to Wiesbaden.

When he finally arrived at Ems, he was shown to a rather squalid hotel room, and was left unpacking his baggage, when the landlady rushed in saying, 'Had I but known! *Freischütz! Preciosa!* I'll turn every soul out into the streets!' Next came a whole succession of other guests, each willing to give up his room: one gentleman brought his luggage with him, already packed, and Weber found himself transferred to the state apartments of the hotel.

At dinner, his health was drunk with much shouting and cheering; the band struck up with an air from *Der Freischütz*, and Weber – whose only desire was to be left alone and in peace – had to sneak out as quietly as he could. He wrote: 'I could almost curse the hour I even composed a note. There is no escape from my own confounded self!'

Weber was dragged around from party to party, forced to improvise dances, or to waltz with a princess. He found the social rounds extremely taxing, but he was especially glad to receive a visit from Charles Kemble and Sir George Smart, who called in to discuss the progress of *Oberon*. His confidence restored, Weber left Ems on 20 August and, on returning to Dresden, began to put Spontini's *Olympia* into rehearsal. This was a diplomatic move, designed to soften Spontini's opposition in Berlin, and it worked. Even though his opera failed in Dresden, Spontini no longer stood in the way of Weber in his efforts to stage *Euryanthe* in the Prussian capital.

So at last, on 5 December 1825, Weber set out to supervise rehearsals in Berlin. As they progressed, he was surprised to see his Dresden superior, Lüttichau, turning up at the theatre. This gentleman, in turn, was surprised to see the kind of homage and respect accorded Weber, not only by men of the highest intellect, but of the most distinguished birth, too. 'Is it possible?' he asked. 'Then, Weber, you really are a celebrated man.'

On 23 December, the Berlin première of *Euryanthe* took place, to great acclaim. But, as in Vienna, the success was to be short-lived: by the fifth performance, the house was empty.

Before he left Berlin, Weber received a contract from Charles

Kemble. *Oberon* was to be premièred at Covent Garden, and Weber would receive five hundred pounds for the English performance rights. This sum was less than Weber had hoped for, but he signed, saying:

It's all the same. Whether I stay or whether I go, in one year I'll be dead anyway. But if I go, my children will have bread when their father dies; if I remain, they will starve.

In this mood, Weber put all his affairs in order prior to departure. His personal appearance had changed for the worse – his posture became bent, his voice weak, his cough incessant. He would fall asleep at odd moments during the day. But he still insisted on going, and, after a heart-rending farewell to his wife and family, set out with the flautist Fürstenau, who had arranged to accompany him.

At times the journey seemed to invigorate Weber – life in France, and in particular French cooking, delighted him, and he arrived in Paris in good spirits. He visited and was visited by, amongst others, Auber, Cherubini and Rossini; whenever he went to the theatre there was a standing ovation in his honour; in general, so much fuss was made of him that Weber wished he had travelled incognito.

On the bitterly cold morning of 2 March, Weber left Paris and headed for Calais. There he took the first packet boat for Dover, where he was greeted by a revenue officer claiming that he'd been instructed to receive Herr Weber with the greatest respect, and that his baggage needn't be examined in the usual way.

Weber was delighted by the journey to London. He wrote:

We dashed along like lightning, through a country charming beyond all description. The meadows are of the loveliest green, the gardens full of bright flowers, and all the houses of an elegance and neatness, which contrast in the most incredible way with the dirt of France.

On 5 March, they arrived in London.

Chapter 19

London

Once in London, Weber went straight to his new home: Sir George Smart's house in Great Portland Street. He recounts:

Here, in Smart's house I am excellently well taken care of. Every possible comfort is provided – there is a bathroom in the house. We dined at six; and by ten o'clock I was in my good bed, where I slept charmingly till seven. Fürstenau is lodged close by. I found a host of visiting-cards awaiting my arrival. One of the first pianoforte-makers has provided me with an admirable instrument . . . I am allowed to be alone the whole day until five; then we dine and go to the theatre, or into society . . . My solitude in England in no way oppresses me. English life and manners are thoroughly sympathetic to my nature; and my little bit of English, in which I am making tremendous progress, is of incredible advantage to me. The English delight in hearing me speak the language . . . People are all so good to me with their anxious care. No king can be served with greater love and affection in all things than I am . . . To show you how undisturbed I am, I will now describe the house. Smart lives on the ground floor, and there, too, is the dining-room. On the first-floor are the reception rooms, and on the second my bedroom and study, where no-one is allowed to come without being announced. People are sent away without ceremony if I cannot see them; and nobody takes this ill. A servant and his wife, whom Smart has had with him 16 years, wait on me to perfection. I cannot be sufficiently grateful to Heaven for the blessings which surround me.

Soon after settling in, Weber was taken off by Sir George Smart to have a look at the Covent Garden Theatre. The piece being given that night was *Rob Roy*, but rumour had got around that Weber would be in the house that night, so more attention was focused on the manager's box than on the stage. Weber, naturally enough, had no inkling of this, and when he arrived went straight to the front of the box, to get a better look at the house. 'There's Weber! There's Weber!', the audience cried, and the performance of *Rob Roy* had to be interrupted as the orchestra struck up the overture to *Der Freischütz*. Weber was over-

Weber, painted by John Cawse in 1826.

whelmed. Writing to Caroline he was incredulous: 'Could it be that the English, who are generally assumed to be so cold, would receive me like this?'

The interpolation of overtures and songs into dramatic spectacles was common in English theatres at this time. The celebrated tenor, Braham, had inserted popular but irrelevant songs and polkas into *Der Freischütz* when it was given at the Lyceum in 1824; far from being put off, the audience delighted in the show all the more, and it was a tremendous success.

Weber could not but disapprove of such tinkering with his music. Nevertheless, he was very happy with the standard of playing and singing that he found in Covent Garden.

139

Portrait of Sir George Smart
by W. Bradley.

Miss Paton is a singer of the very first order, and will sing my Rezia divinely; Braham no less so, although in quite a different style. There are other very good tenors in the company; and I cannot understand what people mean by abusing English singing. The singers display a perfectly good Italian school, and have fine voices, with considerable expression. The orchestra is not very remarkable, but is good enough; and the choruses are excellent. In short, I feel I need have no fears as to the result of my *Oberon* . . . I went afterwards to a concert in Hanover Square Rooms, where all the first Italian singers, Veluti among others, sang. But Miss Paton, who came in after the theatre, and sang a grand air, beat them all hollow.

Weber's first official appearance at Covent Garden was as successful as his impromptu one. In addition to *Oberon*, he had been contracted to conduct four oratorio concerts for the sum of one hundred pounds, and as he was led up to the stage at the start of the opening event, the audience rose and gave him a standing ovation lasting a quarter of an hour. Eventually Weber could begin the concert, which he conducted with a roll of paper held in his right hand, in the German manner. Extracts from *Der Freischütz* went down well, but many people had noticed that Weber coughed a lot during the concert, and next day Sir George Smart's house was inundated with jellies, sweets, lozenges and other remedies given by anxious fans.

The London air might have been bad for Weber's chest, but he found the food agreeable. 'The meat is excellent', he wrote to his wife, 'and the oysters! In Germany, we have never seen such oysters!'

The Admiralty, London.

140

Weber was well looked after by Sir George Smart's family, and he saw a lot of a small circle of admirers, including Charles Kemble and the pianist Ignaz Moscheles. But he did not venture into society and was not taken up to any great degree by the English aristocracy. This was, of course, to his disadvantage: musicians at this time made quite a lot of their income by going from house to house giving concerts. Anyhow, much of his time was taken up with rehearsals for *Oberon*. The singers were good and Weber was particularly taken with the sets and costumes.

Inevitably, there were compromises to be made: Braham didn't

Representation of *Oberon* after a drawing by Ramberg in 1827.

141

The stage-setting for *Oberon*, designed c. 1830 for the first Munich performance.

like the song he'd been given and wanted a new one. Weber wrote to Caroline:

I hate the whole business, but what is to be done? Braham is the idol of the public; and so I must swallow the bitter potion . . . and I so love my original air. I shall keep it for Germany, you may be very sure!

Eventually, after 16 rehearsals, *Oberon* was ready. But the 'evil star', which Weber imagined had always accompanied him through his life, once again executed its malign influence. Firstly, Miss Paton, his prima donna, lost her child and, consequently, suffered an emotional crisis. As if that wasn't enough, a piece of scenery fell on her head at the dress rehearsal, and she was unable to appear. In addition, the rival opera house at Drury Lane, hoping to confuse the issue and to deflect interest away from Weber's opera, staged its own *Oberon*, a melodrama described by

142

Weber as 'a very stupid affair' and, as such, no very great threat.

However, when, on 12 April, Weber arrived to conduct his own *Oberon*, the theatre was full and expectations were high. Every ticket had been sold weeks before, and the audience was not disappointed. They applauded every number, and gave Weber an uproarious reception as he took his curtain call. All the 12 performances which Weber conducted were successful in this way, but to him they were a trial.

Day by day he felt weaker, and, as he crossed off the days on his calendar, he became more and more anxious to see his family again in Dresden. On 18 April, he wrote:

Today is a day enough to kill one, a thick, dark, dank, yellow fog. It is almost impossible to see without candles. The sun has no rays; it is only a red patch amidst the fog. It is awful. My yearning for Hosterwitz and a bright sky is indescribable. Patience! Patience! Day crawls away after day.

On one of these days, Weber went to see *Aladdin*, an opera by Bishop which the Drury Lane Theatre was staging in the hope of rivalling *Oberon*. Afterwards, he wrote:

Yesterday was a most interesting day for me. It was that of the production of my so-called rival's opera *Aladdin*. Places were difficult to obtain. But a proprietor kindly offered me his box . . . scarcely had I entered it, than the whole house rose and greeted me with the greatest enthusiasm. This, in a strange theatre, and on such a day, gave me the truest evidence of the nation's love . . . The opera itself – well, it lasted four and a half hours – enough to give the best-disposed a surfeit of all operas. The applause at first was great . . . but it gradually dwindled away . . . A very pretty hunting chorus was actually hissed; and in the pit they began whistling that from *Der Freischütz* . . . Bishop was not called; and the opera may be considered a failure.

A London Gin house, 1820.

143

On another occasion, Weber experienced the coarseness of a London mob. At a benefit concert for his tenor, Braham, a riot broke out; the galleries yelled, screamed and hooted throughout the whole concert. No-one could hear the music, and the artists were jeered. Weber was not used to this kind of uproar, and it shattered his confidence in the London public. He was all the more worried as he had begun planning a benefit concert of his own, an event designed to be his crowning success and to bring in a lot of money.

But his health was weak, and he hardly had the strength to dictate his music, let alone write it down. To Caroline he wrote:

That hard trial, my concert, still lies before me. I am good for nothing in such matters now. Who will help me? To be sure, all do – and yet – well, it must be gone through – and then – never more.

As things turned out, the concert was not a success. There were rival attractions, including the Epsom races and a concert given by the Duke of St Albans, at which all the high society of London were present. Furthermore, it was raining. The concert hall in the Argyle Rooms was almost empty. As Max Maria describes:

Weber's friends, who knew what store the poor man set by the success of his concert, were terrified, and awaited his entrance with the greatest anxiety. At last, Weber tottered in, supported by Sir George Smart. He looked around; a bitter, painful smile distorted his features, usually so placid in the midst of every suffering. What comfort could the excellent performance of his *Festival of Peace*, of his overtures to *Oberon* and *Euryanthe* hold for him now? What admirable exertions of Braham, Sapio, and Phillips; of Miss Paton, who sang his air to *Atalia* with so much artistic power; of Miss Stephens, who warbled his last song to the words of Moore? The enthusiastic applause of the scanty assembly failed to cheer the heart of the dying man. After the last note of the overture to *Euryanthe*, Fürstenau led him from the room. He fell upon a sofa in an utterly shattered state, almost breathless, and in despair. Friends, musicians, artists around him: but he gave little heed. He only murmured with faint voice, 'What do you say to that? That is Weber in London!'

After this, Weber had only one main aim – to get back to Dresden to see his family before he died. He wrote letters to Caroline, saying that he should be back by June. 'How will you receive me?' he asked. 'In heaven's name, alone. Let no one disturb my joy of looking again upon my wife, my children, my dearest and best . . . Thank God! The end of all is fast approaching.'

Weber's departure was fixed for 6 June 1826, but, by the 4th, it was obvious to everybody that he was too ill to undertake the

The pianist, Ignaz Moscheles.

journey. He spent the evening with Smart, Fürstenau and Moscheles, and retired to bed at around 10.00 pm, refusing to have anyone watch by his bedside, and locking his bedroom door as usual.

Early next morning, when Weber's servant knocked on the door, just as he always did, he received no answer.

He knocked again, louder, becoming more and more anxious. He knew that Weber was always a light sleeper and should have heard him by now. He called for Sir George Smart, and together they forced open the door. Weber was dead. Max Maria informs us that 'not the slightest trace of pain or suffering was visible on his noble features.'

A doctor was summoned; in his opinion Weber had died of consumption, complicated by an ulcer in the throat. Sir George Smart took charge of Weber's affairs; he was amazed at how carefully Weber had prepared for the end, tidying up his belongings and putting money intended for the servants in packets, each carefully sealed and labelled.

The body was embalmed and, on 21 June – some two weeks

Weber on the night of his death.

145

after the death – it was carried through the streets to the Roman Catholic Chapel of St Mary, Moorfields, for a grandiose funeral ceremony featuring Mozart's Requiem.

Weber's friends did not neglect him on this occasion: the orchestra and choruses of Covent Garden, Drury Lane and the Philharmonic Society all offered their services, and the solo rôles were taken by those who had sung in *Oberon*. After the last notes of the Requiem had melted away, the coffin was lowered into a vault; the lights were extinguished and, in an alien environment far from home, the body of Carl Maria von Weber found its first resting place.

It was not until 15 years later, after an article on the subject had been published in the German periodical, *Europa*, that a movement was formed to transfer the body to Dresden. In October 1844 the necessary permission was obtained; Wagner – by now Weber's successor as *Kapellmeister* at Dresden – took control of the affair, and Meyerbeer made over the proceeds of a Berlin production of *Euryanthe* to finance it.

The coffin arrived in Hamburg on 20 October 1844; to the strains of the funeral march from Beethoven's *Eroica* Symphony, it was loaded onto a small boat to begin its journey up the Elbe. The winter of 1844 was a cold one however; before long the river had frozen over, and it wasn't until December that the remains were brought to their final resting place in Dresden, in the Weber family vault.

Weber's Works

The following list contains much of the music mentioned in the text of the book. However, some of Weber's pieces are seldom heard today and do not contribute significantly to the general enjoyment and understanding of his life and times.

Operas and Singspiels:
Das Waldmädchen (1800)
Peter Schmoll und seine Nachbarn (1801–2)
Rübezahl (1804–5)
Silvana (1808–10)
Abu Hassan (1810–11)
Der Freischütz (1817–21)
Die drei Pintos (1820–21)
Euryanthe (1822–23)
Oberon (1825–26)

Other stage works:
Turandot, Prinzessin von China (Gozzi, trans. Schiller) incidental music (1818)
Preciosa (P.A. Wolff) incidental music (1820)

Sacred choral:
Mass (*Grosse Jugendmesse*) in E flat (1802)
Missa sancta no. 2 (*Jubelmesse*) (1818–19)

Cantatas:
Der erste Ton (1808, revised 1810)
In seiner Ordnung schafft der Herr (1812)
Kampf und Sieg (1815)
L'Accoglienza (1817)
Jubel-Kantata (1818)

Other accompanied choral works:
Trauer Musik (1811)

Other unaccompanied choral works:
Das Turnierbankett (1812)
Leyer und Schwert (1814)

Songs:
'Die Kerze' (1802)
'Wiedersehen' (1804)
'Die gefängenen Sänger' (1816)
'Die freien Sänger' (1816)
'Sehnsucht' (1818)

Orchestral and wind:
Romanza siciliana, flute solo (1805)
Six variations on *A Schüsserl und a Reind'rl'*, viola solo (1806)
Symphony No. 1 in C major (1807)
Symphony No. 2 in C major (1807)
Grand pot-pourri, cello solo (1808)
Andante e Rondo ungarese, viola solo (1809)
Piano Concerto No. 1 in C major (1810)
Clarinet Concertino in E flat major (1814)
Clarinet Concerto No. 1 in F minor (1811)
Clarinet Concerto No. 2 in E flat major (1811)
Der Beherrscher der Geister overture (1811)
Bassoon Concerto in F major (1811, revised 1822)
Piano Concerto No. 2 in E flat major (1812)
Horn Concertino in E minor (1806, revised 1815)
Jubel-Ouvertüre
Konzertstück, piano solo (1821)

Chamber music:
Piano Quartet in B flat major (1809)
Seven variations on a theme from *Silvana* for clarinet and piano (1811)
Clarinet Quintet in B flat major (1815–16)

Piano:
Sechs Fughetten (1798)
Six variations on an original theme (1800)
Huit variations sur l'air de ballet de Castor et Pollux [Vogler's opera] (1804)
Momento capriccioso (1808)
Grande Polonaise (1808)
Sonata No. 1 in C major (1812)
Air russe (Schöne Minka) (1815)
Sonata No. 2 in A flat major (1816)
Sonata No. 3 in D minor (1816)
Sonata No. 4 in E minor (1819–22)

Select Bibliography

Abraham, Gerald: 'Weber as Novelist and Critic', *Music Quarterly*, xx, 1934

Benedict, Julius: *Weber*, London, 1881, 5/1899

Cox, H. and C. eds.: *Leaves from the Journals of George Smart*, London, 1907

Foster, Myles Birket: *The History of the Philharmonic Society of London (1813–1912)*, London, 1912

Jähns, Friedrich Wilhelm: *Carl Maria von Weber: eine Lebensskizze nach authentischen Quellen*, Leipzig, 1873

Jullien, Adolphe: 'Weber Paris en 1826', *Revue et gazette musicale*, xxxv (1877)

Obituary, *Quarterly Musical Magazine and Review*, viii (1826), 121

Schönzeler, H.-H. ed.: *Of German Music*, London, 1976

Warrack, John: 'Carl Maria von Weber', *The New Grove Dictionary of Music and Musicians*, ed. S. Sadie, 1980

Warrack, John: *Carl Maria von Weber*, Cambridge University Press, 1976

Weber, Max Maria: *Carl Maria von Weber: ein Lebensbild*, I–II, Leipzig, 1864–86, abridged 2/1912, ed. R. Pechel; Eng. Trans., abridged, London, 1865, photo. repr. 1968

Weston, Pamela: *Clarinet Virtuosi of the Past*, Robert Hale, London, 1971

Index

Illustrations are indicated in **bold** type.

151